WATSONVILLE

Volume II

WATSONVILLE

Memories That Linger

Volume II

by
Betty Lewis

SANTA CRUZ, CALIFORNIA
1980

Pictures courtesy of the Pajaro Valley Historical Association unless otherwise noted.

Special thanks to Elmer, Eddie and Tom Skillicorn; Tim Arano, Sue Manville, Joe Arce, George Menasco, Mitchie Miyamoto, Carl Bronson, Dorothy Erickson, Carlos Rico, Jean Rouse, and Misty Plank.

Copyright © 1980
Valley Publishers
All rights reserved. No part of this book may be reproduced in any form without the written consent of the publisher.
Manufactured in the United States of America.
Valley Publishers
1111 Pacific Avenue
Santa Cruz, California 95060

ISBN 0-934136-08-4
Library of Congress No. 76-41500

*This book is dedicated to Seely Sumpf,
Director, Watsonville Public Library,
whose help, patience, friendship
and interest have been unending—
she makes research a challenge
instead of a chore.*

It's futile to talk too much about the past—something like trying to make birth control retroactive.
                                              Edward Wilson

Preface

We already knew that Betty Lewis was one of the most dedicated, conscientious "local" historians around; now we can add another adjective—prolific.

Having already carved a niche as town historian by virtue of her newspaper articles, historical vignettes for radio and other writings capped by her book, *Watsonville—Memories That Linger*, Mrs. Lewis has written a second volume, another searching look back into the time-stream of events of a century and more ago in the Pajaro Valley.

We're most fortunate Betty picked Watsonville as her home. We doubt that there are many cities of this size which have enjoyed the energetic (and largely unpaid) services and talents of such a person as she.

A town history does more than just record the past for the future. By defining family roots, by tracing the growth of its tradition, and by adding perspective and insights, it gives a community a better sense of its own worth.

In this manner, we welcome Mrs. Lewis' latest look into our past.

Ward Bushee,
Managing Editor,
The Register-Pajaronian

Contents

contents	
Preface	ix
Prologue, Watsonville-1856	xi
Sebastian Rodriguez and the Bolsa Del Pajaro	1
Charles Ford and His Mercantile Store	9
Places and People	21
Chittenden Pass	21
Calaboose and Jail	23
Hecker Pass	24
El Pajaro Springs	25
Corralitos	27
Camp MacQuaide	29
Ralph Wyckoff, Architect	29
Lucius Sanborn	31
Officer John Whalen	42
Skillicorn Baseball Team	33
Thomas Albright	34
Let's Go to the Movies	37
The Small Schoolhouse	51
Ferndale	51
Lindley	51
Amesti	52
Green Valley	53

Carrolton	53
Railroad	57
Beach Road	57
Grace School	58
Houses and Moving Day	61
Fruit Packing Houses	71
Horseless Carriages	81
Businesses	91
Golden Sheaf Flouring Mill	92
Carrie Clausen, Milliner	93
A. Lewis' Packing House	95
Daly Bros.	97
Steinhauser & Eaton	99
Pep Creamery	99
Dr. Charles Butterfield	103
Bicycling Craze	105
James Waters and the Pajaro Valley Nursery	113
Jim Broadis, Runaway Slave	121
Shady Ladies and Sin City	125
And the Rains Came	129
Picture Section	135
Appendix	145
References	146
Index	147

Prologue

Watsonville — 1856

In 1856 the total population of Santa Cruz County was 1,219. There wasn't a newspaper published in Watsonville but local readers could buy the *Pacific Sentinel* which was published in Santa Cruz and sold locally at Ford & Sanborn's store for twenty-five cents a copy or five dollars a year. While most of the news concerned the Santa Cruz area, there was still quite a bit of information about the Pajaro Valley, such as the election for Justice of the Peace—Charles Carter, 203 votes; Godfrey Bockius, 196 votes and for Constable—Thomas Mitchell, 118 votes; R. J. Scott, 121 votes; Bill McDermott, 156 and Bill Fogg, 1 vote.

In June of that year, one-third of the beans and potato crops were destroyed by a severe frost which made for a much leaner winter for the farmers. A new calaboose was being built, funded by private subscription, to house "vagrants who infest the place." On one wild and woolly Saturday night, a drunken Indian stabbed and killed Sacramento Valenzuela, a Sonorian, over on the Monterey side of the Pajaro River—the guilty party was lynched and met with a swift end.

On the brighter side was the opening of the Pacific Exchange Hotel on the site now occupied by the Lettunich Building. Alexander and Billings were the genial proprietors of the new and elegant hostelry with its large and comfortable sleeping rooms, dining room, and nearby stables where horses and buggies were for hire. On September 5 a ball was held at the hotel, and forty gentlemen and more than thirty ladies were in attendance. A tasty supper was followed by sprightly music and couples tripping the light fantastic. "The ladies were handsome and tastily dressed."

Another happening that year was the construction and opening of Brennan's landing where grain and other crops could be stored in the commodious warehouse while waiting to be shipped by boat from the pier. The landing was named after James Brennan a pioneer in the coastal shipping business—he built the *Salinas*, the first steamship to arrive at the landing. Brennan Street is also named for the captain who owned much land around that area of the town. He died in 1885.

That year's Fourth of July celebration, just four years after the town was laid out, was described thusly:

A sumptuous public dinner was prepared, and an arbor of green willows constructed on the public square capable of affording shelter and protection from the heat of the sun, to the large assemblage of ladies and a majority of the gentlemen present. A national salute at sunrise awakened the people of our valley and called them together at 10:00 o'clock A.M. ... The procession after a short march returned to the plaza where the following exercises took place: prayers by Chaplain Rev. J. G. Johnson; reading of Declaration of Independence by Mr. J. W. Sweeny; address to the Spaniards by Mr. Henry Jackson and an oration by P. G. Buchanan. During the intervals the performance of the band was credible and well received by the audience. ... The crowd dispersed; a majority repairing to the races to witness and participate in the exciting sport of the turf....

The literary style in those early years was, to say the least, very colorful and flowery. Somewhere along the line newspaper reporting and the writing of social events became much more mundane. An unknown writer in 1856 described Watsonville's earlier years saying that the first settlement of the Pajaro valley was in 1851 when J. Bryant Hill began farming in the Salsipuedes district on land later owned by the Honorable Jesse D. Carr—the article goes on to say:

The ladies (God bless them) were not then as now a conspicuous element of our population. They were 'like angels' (as usual) and although we designed from the proceeds of our potatoes to erect magnificent mansions; plant gardens; get wives and enjoy in a decent manner the fortunes we were going to make, yet we were then but a community of bachelors, 'ranching' in tents and in crudely built shanties, subsisting upon food such as the patriotic Marion in his courtship with liberty. Yet, still, the lady gender is most intolerably in the minority, and I would here invite to our valley the fair immigrants from other regions promising them a hearty and affectionate reception.

—The *Pacific Sentinel*, 1856

Emerging from the canada, the valley of the Pajaro bursts upon the view, and a more beautiful landscape is not to be seen in California. Before us lay an extensive plain, dotted with the neat cottages of the thrifty farmer, in the midst of the valley the silvery stream of the Pajaro may be seen meandering through the grassy meadows, and fields of growing grain, whilst the coast range of mountains stand out in bold relief on the opposite side of the valley; and to the westward lies the blue Pacific. Such was our first view of the Pajaro; on a nearer approach, we find the soil of remarkable fertility, the land is mostly enclosed and under cultivation and we observed growing in the fields wheat, barley, oats, buckwheat, peas, potatoes, turnips and onions, all looking remarkably thrifty considering the unusually dry weather of this spring. Watsonville is a thriving little village situated on the right bank of the Pajaro. The town contains several large and well stocked stores besides boasting of a school house and church . . .

—*Monterey Sentinel*, April 1856

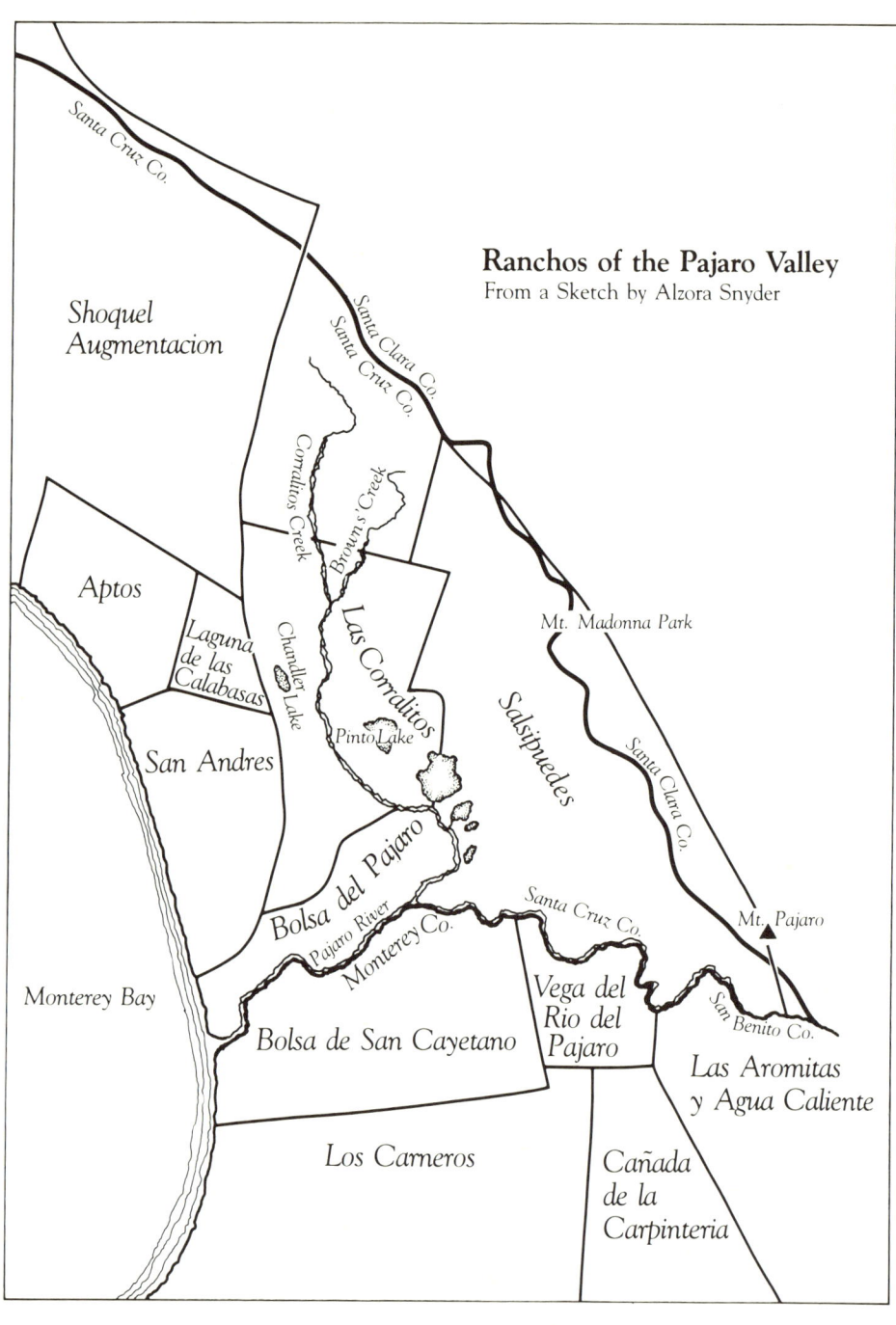

Chapter One

Sebastain Rodriguez and the Bolsa Del Pajaro

Sebastian Rodriguez, son of Jose Antonio Rodriguez and Vicenta de Leon, was the recognized owner of the Bolsa del Rio del Pajaro Rancho in 1823 and 1828 when he was a sergeant in the Monterey presidial company. He leased the land for twenty-five pesos a year to Captain Juan Cooper, who constructed corrals, barns, a house, grist mill, etc. on what is now the north end of Main Street up the hill in the Gonzales Street area. When Sebastian left the army in 1832 Cooper turned the property back to him with all the improvements which had been in their agreement. The small house was replaced by an adobe in 1842 to house Rodriguez's wife, Perfecto Pacheco, and their many children. The house was on high land, so there was good drainage and no problem when the rivers flooded.

This land grant was confirmed to Sebastian in October of 1836 and again in 1837, by Governor Alvarado, to Sebastian and his brother, Alejandro. Along came Judge John Howard Watson in 1852, who, along with Durell Gregory, purchased "all of the one undivided half part of that tract of land—Rancho Bolsa del los Rodriguez"; the price was $400 and this was to be the site of the village of Pajaro, later to be dubbed Watsonville. This land was subdivided and sold off at ten dollars an acre; one of the first purchasers was Otto Stoesser whose business block, which was

Watsonville Plaza, donated by the heirs of Sebastian Rodriguez.

built in 1872 and replaced a wooden structure, is still standing across from the plaza.

Litigation over the Rodriguez land grant was in and out of the courts for years and all the proceedings would fill a large book. The United States District Court confirmed the title in 1860—the Patent was dated January 4, 1860 and signed by President James Buchanan. It was duly recorded on April 16, 1860.

The city plaza was donated to the people of Watsonville by Sebastian, through his heirs, in 1860—eight years before Watsonville was to be incorporated.

From the Santa Cruz County recorder's office—Vol. 1; page 382 of Deeds:

Facundo Rodriguez to Gregory and Watson—Know all men by these present that I Facundo Rodriguez of said county in consideration of the sum of Four hundred dollars paid by John H. Watson and Durell S.

Gregory of said county the receipt whereof is hereby acknowledged do hereby remise, release and forever quit-claim unto the said Watson and Gregory their heirs and assigns forever all right, title, interest, claim or demand that I in anywise have in and to a certain tract of land situated in said county and known as the Rancho de Los Rodriguez or Bolsa del Pajaro containing two square leagues more or less.

To have and to hold the above released premisis with all the priveleges (*sic*) and appertenances (*sic*) thereunto belonging to the said Watson and Gregory their heirs and assigns to them and their use and behoof forever.

In witness whereof the said Facundo Rodriguez has hereunto set his hand and seal this the eighteenth day of August in the year of our Lord eighteen hundred and fifty two.

(signed and sealed) August 18, 1852

Facundo was a brother of Sebastian and, as was shown earlier, did not have legal title to the land.

NAME OF RANCHO	DATE OF GRANT	TO WHOM GRANTED	DATE OF CONFIRMATION BY U.S. DISTRICT COURT	TO WHOM CONFIRMED BY U.S.	NUMBER OF ACRES
Vega del Rio del Pajaro	1820 1833	Antonio Castro	1850	Fred A. McDougal, et al., widower of Mrs. Juan Anzar	4,310.29
Bolsa de San Cayetano	1820 (?) 1824 1834	Ignacio Vallejo Jose Delores Pico Jose de Jesus Vallejo, son	1856	Jose de Jesus Vallejo, son	8,866.43
Canada de Salsipuedes	1823 11/1834 3/1840 1843	Francisco de Hara Manuel Jimeno	1861	Jas. Blair, et al.	31,201.37
Bolsa del Rio del Pajaro	1823 and 1828 10/1836 and 11/1837	Sebastian Rodriguez Sebastian and Alejandro Rodriguez	1860	Sebastian Rodriguez	5,496.50
Los Corralitos	1823 and 1841	Jose Amesti	1861	Jose Amesti	15,440.02
San Andres	11/1833	Joaquin Castro	1876	Guadalupe Castro, eldest son	8,911.53
La Lagune de Las Calabasas	12/1833	Felipe Hernandez	1868	Heirs of Charles Morse	2,304.75
Las Aromitas y Las Aguas Calientes	10/1835	Juan Miguel Anzar	1862	Fred A. McDougal, et al.	8,659.69

By Alzora Snyder

Will of Sebastian Rodriguez

I, Sebastian Rodriguez, native of Alta California, and resident of the Pajaro, State of Cal., and County of Santa Cruz, legitimate son of Antonio Rodriguez and Vicente de Leon, deceased, finding myself, by the grace of God, in good health, and of my sound mind, but fearful of death to which we are all exposed, I make, decree and ordain this my last will and testament in manner and form as follows:

FIRST:—I commend my soul to God, who created it from nothing, and my body to the earth from which it was formed.

Item:—I command there be no pomp at my interment, but that some masses may be said, circumstances permitting.

Item:—I declare that I am married to Perfecta Pacheco, and that during our married life we have by Divine Providence had twelve children, male and female, and they are as follows:—Jose Antonio, Pedro, Jose, Jacinto, Rafaila, Solano, Teresa, Deciderio, Bernabela, Ma. Antonio, Carmen and Ramona.

Item:—I declare that my (sons) (children) Jose Antonio and Rafaila (Rafaelo?) are married and have received the share of personal property which by inheritance belongs to them, and they have no claim at my death further than the share of land which as heirs belongs to them, after the partitions hereinafter mentioned, shall be made.

Item:—I declare that to no person do I owe money or anything of value, and if any claim be made against me it is null and without value, and the persons who owe me will be found in my papers in a list of names and amounts of indebtedness, and when this shall be collected it will be added to the body of my estate.

Item:—I declare that the cattle (*ganado*) and troop of horses (*caballada*) which are in possession of my son, Jacinto, with my brand and mark, are his property, as well as any other res (single head of cattle) which bears the mark or brand of any of my children, for, in order to avoid trouble, we made this exchange, when he took his interest (or share) to put them in the place called "La Posa," and the stock which are in the "Rancho de la Ballena," with brand and mark of my son, Jacinto, belong to me by the exchange referred to in this article.

Item:—I declare it to be my will that there be given to La Salvador four milch cows with heifer calves, for, as I raised her as a daughter, I wish to show her this kindness.

Item:—I declare that the Rancho called Rincon de la Ballena was bought by me and my son Jacinto, and it is my will and command that the said part which Jacinto has in the said Rancho de la Ballena remain to the benefit of my heirs, and that there be delivered to my son Jacinto a half league and a quarter of land in the Rancho de la Bolsa del Pajaro, in recompense for the part of the Rancho de la Ballena, which belonged to

"La Casa Materna" adobe house built by Don Ignacio Vicente Ferrar Vallejo on Werner's Hill, Salinas Road, Monterey County. Built around 1824, it was to be called the "Glass House" because of its many glass windows. The building was torn down in 1962.

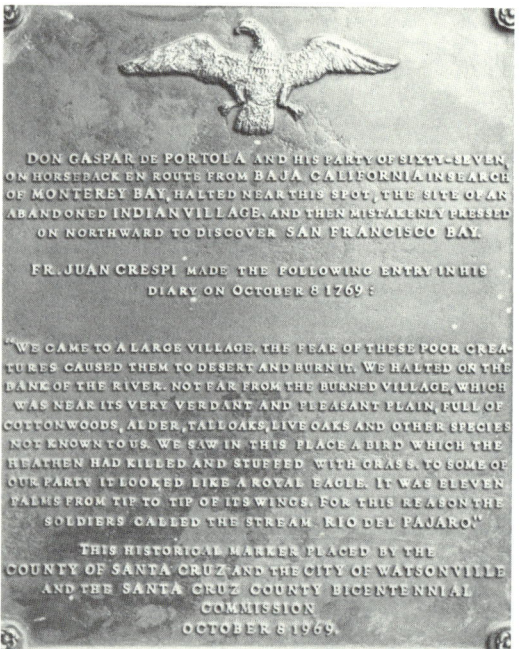

This historical marker is on the bank of the Pajaro River, where Portola and his party stopped in October of 1769. The river divides Monterey and Santa Cruz counties.

him, commencing the measurements of land in the Bolsa del Pajaro for my son Jacinto, on the south side nearest the *Estero* (Tide Water Creek) which is close by the sea, and from thence towards the north, to where comes the whole of the measurement of the half league and a quarter aforesaid.

Item:—I recognize for my property, real and personal, the Rancho called "Rincon de la Ballena," which contains one league, a little more or less, and the Rancho called "Bolsa del Pajaro," which must contain about two leagues scant, excepting the part which my son Jacinto owns in said Rancho, by the exchange which we mutually made between us both, as is expressed in the clause anterior to this.

Item:—I declare that the houses in said Rancho are mine, and the cattle and horses which my heirs recognize as my property.

Item:—I declare it to be my last will that my beloved wife, my sons and daughters be my only and universal heirs, and that my wife enjoy the one-half of all my interests as well property, real as personal.

The house now building in the Rancho Bolsa del Pajaro belongs to my son, Jose, and it is my will to add to it the double quantity of land which falls to my other children in the Rancho de la Ballena, and the rest of all my property, real and personal, shall be divided in equal parts between my said children, Pedro, Jose, Jacinto, Solano, Teresa, Deciderio, Bernabela, Ma. Antonio, Carmen and Ramona, excepting Jose Antonio and Rafaela; since to the last there only remains (belong) their part of the land in the two Ranchos by reason of having already received the part of the stock which by inheritance belongs to them, as already mentioned.

Item:—I name for my executors my wife, Perfecta Pacheco, and my sons, Pedro and Jose, in order that in solidum they will cause this my last will to be complied with, and they may and shall take possession of all my known property, real and personal, immediately upon the occasion of my death, and they may sell the part they deem necessary for funeral and medical expenses or any other necessities without asking permission from the Probate Court nor account to the same. The Judge will please admit this, my Testament, to probate, approve it, and order the issuance of letters of administration to my said Executors, without requiring any kind of bond from them, for they have my entire confidence.

Lastly:—As I, my wife and family have till now lived together in all tranquility and love, I charge and beg them to continue, if possible, so to live, one helping another in guarding the interest which God has given us, and I charge my daughters in particular to watch over their poor mother, to respect and guard the interest belonging to her, rendering her always the honor to which she is entitled, and if they do so, God, our

Lord, will reward them and augment their fortunes, and they will receive His blessings for all time as they already have mine.

And I declare if there be had, or appear in any time, any other Testament, made by me anterior to this I declare it null and of no value, and only this shall have force.

Signed in Monterey, State of California, the 26th day of April, A.D. 1854.

SEBASTIAN RODRIGUEZ.

Sebastian Rodriguez died in 1855.

Chapter Two

Dr. Charles Ford and His Mercantile Store

Messers. Ford & Barney have nearly completed a two-story building—the lower floor of which is to be appropriated to mercantile purposes; the upper floor is designed for a lodge room for the Masonic fraternity, a branch of which order has recently been established here..."

—Pacific *Sentinel,* April 11, 1857

There have been many who have contributed much to the growth and welfare of the Pajaro Valley but there was one man who still stands out today—he seemed to have an extra share of vision, determination, enterprise and a lot of good, common sense. That man was Dr. Charles Ford, founder of the oldest mercantile store in California—City of Paris in San Francisco held that distinction until a few years ago.

Ford was born January 3, 1824 on a farm near New Brunswick, New Jersey. His parents died when he was quite young; Ford also had two brothers and a sister. At the age of fourteen, Charles went to work in a dry goods store where he was to get his first

A 1900 lithograph of the Charles Ford Company building which was erected in 1884.

taste of being a salesman. An apothecary shop was the next place of employment where dispensing drugs and treating the ill were done with regularity. Moving next to New York, Ford acquired two drug stores of his own and was soon dubbed with the title of "doctor." Druggists, in those early years, often performed the duties of a physician or a dentist as medical men were in short supply.

When the news of gold being discovered in California reached the East Coast, Ford decided to head west and boarded the ship *Croton* which sailed via Cape Horn. After 198 days at sea the ship docked at San Francisco—the date was July 31, 1849 and young Ford was twenty-five years old. Journeying to the mining fields in the Yuba River area Charles did quite well for himself, but ill health forced his return to the East Coast but not for long, as he returned to San Francisco in the spring of 1850 and immediately engaged in the mercantile business in a building on Jackson Street.

Charles Ford.

The illustrations in Chapter Two are courtesy of the Charles Ford Company.

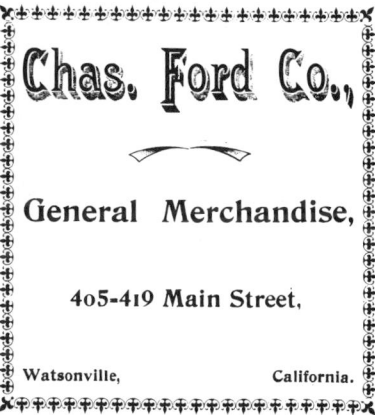

An 1899 advertisement.

The city by the bay was a wild and woolly place at that time and the hastily constructed wooden structures were repeatedly consumed by flames. Fortunes were made and lost at a very rapid rate, in many instances. Charles Ford was one of those who prospered and, while boarding at a lodging house in the city, he heard men speak of the fertile Pajaro Valley and the top prices being paid for the potato crops. He decided to sell his business and try his hand at raising potatoes and, along with three other men, he leased land in the Amesti district and planted 200 acres to spuds.

Unfortunately, the bottom fell out of the market due to overproduction and farmers harvested, sacked and hauled their potatoes to a non-existant market. Charles Ford left his crop rotting on the ground thus saving that expense. His decision was to return to the mercantile business and decided that the Pajaro Valley was a good place to live so he built a one-story wooden structure on Main Street, then called Pajaro Street, next to the Cooper house which was located on the corner of Pajaro and West Third (Beach) streets. The year was 1852. His first partner was a man by the name of Barney.

In 1860 the *Pacific Sentinel* (Watsonville did not have a paper of its own until 1863) reported that Dr. Ford had made a stirring speech in front of the Nebraska Hotel, which was then located across from where City Hall now stands. This was at a Republi-

Ford Block, 1900.

can ratification meeting and he was elected to the State Legislature that same year. The following appeared in the *Sentinel* in April of 1861:

Dr. Ford, our representative in the Legislature, paid us a flying visit last week. The Dr. had been suffering from a somewhat severe illness in Sacramento, and came down to try the virtues of Santa Cruz air and water.

Ford served one term as Assemblyman and was never to run for political or public office again. Ill-health plagued him all his life and he took many trips to try and restore his health traveling to such distant places as South America, Europe, Hawaii and back to the East Coast. He first lived at Scott's Boarding House on Union Street, now the site of Valley National Bank, and sat down to dinner of an evening with such men as Judge Watson, Jesse D. Carr, Captain James Brennan and Otto Stoesser.

Charles remained a bachelor all his life though the story has been handed down that he had a mistress who lived on Rodriguez Street—some say she is buried up at Pioneer Cemetery in the Ford plot.

In 1865 Lucius Sanborn became Ford's bookkeeper and, at the end of his first year of employment he was given half of the business as his "fair share." The name was changed to Ford & Sanborn:

Messers Ford & Sanborn have lately improved their store by tearing away the partition which divided the building; thus making one large room. They have now a fine commodius place of business and with their roomy storehouses, lumber yard, etc., have the most extensive establishment in this part of the county.
       —The *Pajaronian*, August 20, 1868

Ford's lumber mill was up above Corralitos where twenty teams would be used for hauling split lumber down to Watsonville and other nearby towns. In 1871, when Southern Pacific laid track from Gilroy to Pajaro, the mill supplied the railroad with 50,000 railroad ties. In a two-year period between April 1, 1880 and April 1, 1882, the lumber company shipped, from the depot, 2,960 cars of lumber—this was an average of nearly five cars per day excluding Sunday. The lumber yard was located in back of the store and there was also a yard over in Pajaro.

The Ford and Sanborn Company building in King City.

Ford's at Main and West Beach in 1969.

In 1873 the old wooden store was moved off the Ford property on Main Street and a two-story brick building was constructed which was designed by Alex Chalmers. Sanborn retired from the business in 1879, and A. A. Morey and James Sidney Menasco were taken into the firm and the name was changed to Charles Ford & Company.

Dr. Ford leased Pajaro Landing in 1881 (now the site of Pajaro Dunes South) and named it Camp Goodall. Soon buildings were being constructed including a hotel, cottages, race track, restaurant, dancing pavilion, etc. This became a popular summer resort where fishing was good and the ladies could step into one of the wooden bath houses and be wheeled down to the water's edge, stepping into the cold water from their conveyance ... squealing all the way!

Another view of Ford's, taken in 1901.

His other business interests included Ford & Sanborn's in Salinas and King City; Paraiso Springs near Soledad; land in San Jose and, it is said that at one time he owned one-fourth of the town of Watsonville. A new Ford's store was built in 1883. It was also designed by Alex Chalmers and measured eighty-four feet in length, twenty-six feet in width, and sixteen and one-half feet high. Next to it were located, facing on Main Street, a brick warehouse and two grain warehouses. This same year Ford

Just before the tower was removed in 1925, during the remodeling.

Ford's in 1925, after the corner steeple had been removed and the lower portion "modernized."

purchased the Cooper property on the corner next to his store and the house was moved back to Rodriquez and the following year a new Ford Block was erected designed by Jacob Lenzen of San Jose. The two-story edifice had office suites on the second floor—the bay window suite being rented by Dr. Charles Butterfield, dentist.

In 1888 the Spreckels Sugar Factory was built in Watsonville and Charles Ford was very instrumental in bringing this about which did much to help the sagging economy in the valley. Another happening at the store in 1888 is shown below:

Charles Ford & Co. are about to introduce a cash system in their mercantile establishment, which is similar to that in general use in large retail stores in San Francisco. Under this system all cash will be received by a cashier (and for this position Miss Daisy Longley, a young lady of Santa Cruz who has had experience in such a position has been selected) and to save customers from settling at the cashier's office the coin will be sent in boxes run on wires, and the change (if any) and bill returned the same way. The wires are being put in this week.
—The *Pajaronian*, April 26, 1888

Ford's in 1954. The lower portion had been modernized and a three-story building added to the right.

The office of Ford's in the 1920s. Sid Menasco is in the middle at the back. Claude Irish is on the stool to the right.

Ford's employees picnic—June 13, 1915.

Presidents of Ford's over the years have been Charles Ford, Lucius Sanborn, J. S. Menasco, H. D. Tuttle, S. T. Menasco, Victor Tuttle, and the current president, George Tuttle Menasco. George's grandfather, better known as Sid Menasco, started clerking at Ford's in 1875 and, in 1890, he became the general manager of the newly incorporated Charles Ford Company. He married Mary Tuttle in 1874 and they had two children, Sidney and Edna. Sid died in 1909 after having become president in 1906. His son, also called Sid, was president and general manager at the time of his death in 1932; George became president in 1967.

Cooper house stood on the corner of Main and West Beach. Ford's purchased the property in 1883 and extended their store to the corner.

The store was to change its face many times over the years, all the while expanding and growing. Ralph Wyckoff and William Weeks designed some of the buildings—it was in 1929 that a third story was built onto the northern part of the store; in 1956 a third story on the southern section. Branch stores were added in Santa Cruz, Hollister, Salinas and Gilroy and more property was purchased in Watsonville to secure better parking.

Charles Ford died on November 16, 1890 at the age of sixty-five—his estate was valued at $500,000—no small sum ninety years ago. Many people were remembered in his will including his faithful servant, Ah Moon. The largest monetary bequest of $10,000 went to a Spanish woman in San Jose, but many local people were remembered for their service or thoughtful acts. The following is from the local paper at the time of Ford's death:

Soon after midnight last Friday night, Dr. Charles Ford breathed his last at his house on Third Street and the long, busy and useful life of Pajaro Valley's foremost citizen was ended. The funeral took place on Sunday afternoon under the management of the Pajaro Lodge. Long before the time set for the funeral the streets near the Ford cottage were crowded with vehicles while the sidewalks were thronged with people. The Masons and the Watsonville Fire Department led the funeral line, and over 150 vehicles were in the procession that followed the remains to the cemetery. The funeral was the largest ever witnessed in the valley. He was a man of strong convictions, one who expressed himself forcibly and who acted upon his convictions.

According to local legend, after the burial service the local band marched back into town playing the lively tune "Ta-ra-ta-boom-de-ay" thus honoring Ford's last request. Charles Ford certainly left his mark on the Pajaro Valley as well as other nearby communities—a personable man with a good sense of humor and an exceptionally keen mind—he very obviously had a definite flair for the business world and wouldn't he be truly amazed to see what that business has turned into—I'm sure he would.

The mammoth establishment of this firm (Ford's) is divided into five distinct departments, the systematic arrangement of which, and the admirable manner in which the various goods are displayed, betraying the presence of an experienced and master hand. The five stores are especially well lighted and ventilated, and the goods have a clean, bright and fresh appearance. The same is to be said of the furniture store, which is in a separate building, and which is under the management of F. A. Kilburn, representing Dr. Ford, who alone is proprietor of this branch of the business.

The visitor to the grocery department of Charles Ford & Co. cannot fail to be impressed by its size, and that of the stock of staple and fancy goods, in both of which respects it resembles a first-class San Francisco establishment, rather than what would be expected in a city the size of Watsonville....

—*Pacific Coast Commercial Record*, San Francisco,
January 10, 1890

Chapter Three

Places and People

CHITTENDEN PASS

Chittenden Road runs through land that once belonged to a San Francisco lawyer by the name of Nathanial W. Chittenden. In 1882 the local paper was noting that the roads on Mr. Chittenden's ranch were the most extensive, costly and the best to be found in that section. His law partner was a man by the name of Robert Simmon and when Chittenden died in 1885, while staying at the

Bill Cumming, Fred Wilson and Louis Lopes motoring out Chittenden Road, in a Buick White Streak, before it was paved in 1920. Courtesy Allen Lopes.

Albert Snyder and his dog Carlo, driving on Chittenden Pass Road, c. 1916. Courtesy Albert Snyder.

Chittenden Road prior to 1920.

Mansion House Hotel, he left his large estate to his partner. Nathanial had no immediate family and his relatives back east were not mentioned in the Holographic will which consisted of just fifty-one words. Soon, these relatives were contesting the will saying that Mr. Simmon had used undue influence over the recently departed. In May of 1886, eighteen months after Chittenden's death, the case was settled with the relatives receiving the estate and paying Mr. Simmon a sum of $45,000. A nephew of Chittenden, Talman Chittenden, was appointed administrator of the estate and, in 1887, the vast land holdings were surveyed and a portion of the property was divided into twenty-acre lots and sold. In 1894 the county accepted the Chittenden Road as a public highway. The road was paved in 1920 for $18,005.

CALABOOSE AND JAIL

When Watsonville was just going through its birthing pains, enforcement of the law was very often a haphazard business at best. There were no jails so prisoners had to be tied to the nearest tree or pole or placed in a hotel room under guard. According to the *Pacific Sentinel*, in 1856, the citizens of Watsonville had raised enough money by public subscription to build a calaboose, the informal word for prison.

Ten years later, another notice appeared in the newspaper: "Let us have a calabozo—strange as it may seem, it is nevertheless true that petty offenders are let run at large for want of some place of confinement, and drunken travelers, for the same reason, exercise undue license in disturbing the quiet of the village." It is not known what happened to that first jail, maybe it burned down. Nevertheless, in 1869 a new structure was built measuring sixteen by twenty-four feet. "No more will boozy individuals be obliged to stretch their trembling limbs in the cold, cold gutter, but lodgings will hereafter be furnished them. There is only one drawback to the place. Those who patronize the institution are obliged to pay an outrageous price for their lodgings but there are no sweets without the bitter."

The Town Trustees have offered $200 reward for the arrest and conviction of the party or parties who set fire to the Calaboose last Sunday night.

—*The Pajaronian,* January 25, 1877

A new jail was built, designed by James Waters, and A. Lewis and Company provided the blankets at a cost of twelve dollars.

In 1878 the following appeared in the *Pajaronian:* "At the special meeting of the town trustees, an ordinance providing for a chain gang was ordered drafted. All criminals sentenced to the calaboose will have to work out their sentences in the chain gang. This is a good move, and plenty of work can be found on the streets for all dwellers at the Hotel de Knevels (constable)."

In 1913 a new jail was built on Rodriguez Street, replacing one that stood behind the old city hall on Main Street, forerunner of the present facilities built in 1936 on Union Street.

HECKER PASS

What we now know as Hecker Pass Highway was once called Bodfish Canyon Road after a Mr. Bodfish who owned land atop Mt. Madonna. He conducted a logging operation and it developed that he had appropriated a section of timber belonging to the Salsipuedes Grant and a lengthy litigation followed. A committee comprised of Salsipuedes ranch owners journeyed up the hill to meet with Bodfish who had brought along a delicious lunch for all which included chicken, turkey and iced champagne. He later claimed that he won his right to adjust the property lines by goading the appetites of the committee—he would not distribute the contents of the picnic basket until the discussion was finalized—in his favor!

Hecker Pass Highway was opened to the public on May 27, 1928 and more than 2,000 automobiles chugged up to the summit for the festivities which included speech-making and a hearty picnic lunch. Ten years later, in 1938, Henry Hecker, Santa Clara County Supervisor from Gilroy, was guest of honor at a barbecue up at Mt. Madonna. A bronze plaque was unveiled at the summit bearing the following inscription:

This testimonial is dedicated to Henry Hecker, whose foresight made possible the completion of the Yosemite-to-the-Seas Highway, May 27, 1928.

EL PAJARO SPRINGS

Watsonvillians have found various places in the past for their recreational pleasure—among the favorite spots were Tassajara Hot Springs, Paraiso Hot Springs, Gilroy Hot Springs and, closer to home, El Pajaro Springs out on Chittenden Road which was also called St. Francis Springs and Chittenden Springs. At one time it was owned by the St. Francis Hospital in San Francisco and was used by the Brothers as a summer retreat. There was also a chicken ranch and vegetable garden from which supplies were trucked up to the city to be used at the hospital.

But before this, back in July of 1906, the following appeared in the *Evening Pajaronian:*

To establish a summer resort—during his visit this morning, A. F. Martel, president of the Market Street Bank of San Francisco, stated that

Buildings at St. Francis Springs. The building in back has been torn down. The one to the left was once the post office, is now a rental.
Courtesy Dorothy Erickson

it is his intention to begin immediately the establishing of a summer resort at Chittenden. He has acquired the handsome home property of Talman Chittenden and will begin preparing the several sulphur springs for use. The quality of these springs together with their great variety makes it an easy task to utilize their properties in building up a reputation for such a resort as is planned by Mr. Martel. A large hotel and numerous summer cottages are to be built, the springs will be cleaned out and their flow increased and conserved, and it is among the possibilities that a dam will be constructed in the Pajaro river to hold the water for a summer lake for boating parties...

A handsome brochure was published entitled "For recreation, health and pleasure, go to El Pajaro Springs, Chittenden, Ca., George Sully, Jr., manager." This vacation spot offered hot sulphur baths, cozy cottages, a fine new dance hall, and a new hotel with fourteen beautiful rooms plus a dining hall, located amid the elms and cypress trees. It was in 1918 that the St. Francis Brothers purchased the springs, but they sold the resort in April of 1923, as shown by the following item which appeared in the *Pajaronian:*

The St. Francis Springs at Chittenden owned and conducted for several years past by the Franciscan Order, was sold by the order, yesterday to Clark and Holland, well-known in Sonoma County, where they conducted a summer resort at Monte Rio.

El Pajaro Springs. Courtesy Dorothy Erickson.

But the resort was never to attain any great degree of popularity even though it was readily accessible by auto or train and offered many inducements shown by the following description. "The property comprises thirty-five acres of wooded grounds, situated at the foot of the mountains, with the beautiful Pajaro River winding its way through the property in limpid beauty."

Located nearby was the Chittenden RR Station and post office plus the hotel which, at one time, was used for the Southern Pacific workers until they were moved over to Aptos. Robert and Dorothy Erickson purchased the property in 1964 and live in the old hotel, or chalet as it was sometimes called. A few of the old buildings have survived but most of that early-day resort has faded into the past.

CORRALITOS NOTES

This is the name of an embryo town destined, at some future day, to be of some importance to Santa Cruz County. It is situated on the Corralitos ranch, about six miles from Watsonville, near the place where the Corralitos creek debouches from the mountains. There is one grist mill, two stores, a wagon and blacksmith shop, a school house, some twenty dwelling houses, and others going up. The village is the resort of lumbermen. There are three saw mills a few miles up the creek, above the town. The village wears a cheerful and busy aspect, and, if we are not much mistaken, will soon be a rival of Soquel for the honor of the County seat. Hurrah for Corralitos.
—*Pacific Sentinel*, February 7, 1861

Spring Meeting over the Watsonville course—Five days racing—We had the pleasure of visiting the track, a few miles from Watsonville, near Corralitos, one day the present week. The track is situated on a beautiful flat, the portion selected for the spectators being embowered with the giants of the forest, the old oak trees. Accommodations for ladies, away from the noisy rabble, is nicely arranged with comfortable seats in the shade and a fine view of the track, which is of a circular form of one mile. The proprietors of the track kindly showed us the candidates for the honor of the turf and we can say with truth, we never saw horses in better trim. There are at least fifteen or twenty animals at this camp of instruction, all blooded stock, going through a regular "course of sprouts."

—Pajaro Valley *Times*, May 12, 1866

A gang of Watsonville would-be bloods went to Corralitos Saturday night and made fools of themselves by acting in the way they did. Their behavior would put to shame a Tar Flat hoodlum of San Francisco, who are gentlemen beside these three or four Watsonville hoodlums. And what is worse these boys would like to have people believe they belonged to the elite of Watsonville. We understand that if anything occurs again similar to that of Saturday night, these gentlemen (?) will find themselves in the hands of the law.

—*Watsonville Daily Register*, June 13, 1895

Church at Camp McQuaide (now Monterey Bay Academy) during World War II.

CAMP McQUAIDE

On the site of the Monterey Bay Academy, San Andreas Road, was once the army site named Camp McQuaide in honor of Major Joseph P. McQuaide who was a popular Catholic Chaplain; a graduate of Santa Clara University. One million dollars was appropriated for the camp by February of 1941 and a one hundred bed hospital and post theatre were soon completed. The 664-acre army post housed nearly 2,000 military prisoners during World War II and was a training camp for such outfits as the 250th Coast Artillery, 64th Signal Corps, 76th Cavalry, 154th Medics, and the U.S. Naval Radar Unit.

In April of 1947, the military prisoners were transferred out of the camp; most of them going to Camp Cooke, and soon afterwards, the use of Camp McQuaide as a military base was terminated and the property transferred from the army to the war assets administration—the army had declared the post surplus. The following appeared in the *Register Pajaronian* on June 28, 1948: "Camp McQuaide probably will become a school under auspices of the Seventh Day Adventist Church. The government will make a virtual gift of the camp site to the Central California Conference of Seventh Day Adventists." And thus, Monterey Bay Academy.

RALPH WYCKOFF, ARCHITECT

Ralph Wyckoff was born in Watsonville in 1884, the son of Cyrus Newton Wyckoff, local engineer. Ralph attended local schools and, afterward, went to work in the office of William Weeks as a draftsman along with his brother, Frank. After studying architecture in Paris, Ralph received his California license to practice in 1914. In 1915 he returned to Watsonville, after conducting his own office in Berkeley, and took over the business of architect H. B. Douglas. Wyckoff designed such buildings as the Radcliff School, Woman's Club, the present fire station, remodeling of Ford's department store, and a number of local homes.

In 1919 he moved to Salinas with his wife, the former Myrtle Cornell, where he opened an office and became associated with

Ralph Wyckoff designed the Watsonville fire station, which is on Second Street, in 1925, and an addition to it in 1927.

Watsonville Woman's Club building was designed by Ralph Wyckoff in 1917. It is located at 12 Brennan Street.

architect Hugh C. White. Mr. Wyckoff designed the present Salinas High School, remodeled the Ford & Sanborn store, and was responsible for many of the buildings at Hartnell Junior College. 1921 saw the family moving to San Jose where Wyckoff worked with White until 1925, when the partnership was dissolved. Mr. White went to Oakland and Wyckoff stayed in San Jose, where he died in August of 1956 at the age of seventy-two, having designed a number of buildings in that city including the post office and structures at San Jose State University.

LUCIUS SANBORN

Lucius Sanborn was born in Maine in 1824 and grew up with a love for the sea; when still a young lad, he could equip and command a vessel with ease and dexterity. In July of 1849 he arrived in California coming to the Pajaro Valley in 1852 and opening up a blacksmith shop on what was then known as Pajaro Street—the main thoroughfare through town.

Lucius Sanborn was born in 1824 and died in 1899. At one time he was a partner in and president of the Charles Ford Company. Courtesy George Menasco.

In 1865 he went to work in Charles Ford's mercantile store and, after a year's time, Mr. Ford made him a partner and the firm's name was changed to Ford & Sanborn. Lucius suffered from asthma throughout his life and his business interests, which included the Ford store in Salinas, got to be too much of a burden on his health so he retired from the local store in 1879. After Ford's death in 1890, Sanborn returned and served as president of the firm.

Sanborn was married to Carrie Scott and they had two children—Nellie, who married the honorable S. W. Backus of San Francisco and Lucius W., a businessman in Salinas. When Mr. Sanborn died in 1899, a friend wrote—"He was a good man, a kind friend, a worthy citizen, beloved by those who knew him best—when a good man dies, the people mourn."

OFFICER JOHN WHALEN

On the night of October 25, 1920 the body of officer John Whalen was found on the city lot in back of the auditorium on Second Street—he had been shot five times. Earlier, Whalen had arrested a man by the name of Fred Pena who was drunk and disturbing the peace in front of the California Restaurant, 259 Main Street. The officer and the accused walked off towards the jail, then located on Rodriguez Street, and soon gun shots were heard and reported to the authorities by a man who had witnessed the arresting of Pena.

Sheriff Trafton, Chief of Police Whitsitt and Constable Devin, after finding Whalen's body, went out looking for the prisoner and found him at a home up on Watsonville Heights where he was then taken into custody. Pena claimed he was not guilty and had gone to bed early that evening. A few days later he confessed to the crime over at the county jail saying he and Whalen had known each other for years but that there had been bad feelings between them for some time. He was sentenced to twenty-five years at San Quentin prison and, after serving his time, he returned to Watsonville for a short period and then moved on to Fresno where he died.

Officer Whalen was seventy years old at the time of his death; he had moved to Watsonville from Castroville in 1905 and in those last fifteen years had become very well liked in Watsonville. His killer came very close to being strung to the nearest tree before being taken away to jail.

SKILLICORN BASEBALL TEAM

Watsonville has had many claims to fame but one of the most interesting was the Skillicorn baseball team which played exhibition games in the early 1920's. It started out as a joke when one of

Skillicorn brothers' baseball team—1922. Left to right: Top Row, William Lee, third base; George Edward, first base; George Edward, Sr.; Clarence Douglas, catcher; John Archie ("Kilwee"), left field; Middle Row, Arthur Edwin (Eddie), shortstop; Thomas Henry (Harry), pitcher; Bottom Row, Walter Lewis Amos (Amos), second base; Kenneth Albert (Albert), center field; Richard Elmer (Elmer), right field. The brothers played several practice games in 1921 and came out in uniform in 1922. Their picture was placed in the Baseball Hall of Fame in 1961. Courtesy Eddie Skillicorn.

the nine Skillicorn brothers told the manager of the Watsonville Pippin baseball team that he and his brothers could whip the hometown team. Most of the boys worked on the railroad and came all decked out in overalls for their first games. The team was managed by their father, George "Pop" Skillicorn and the four girls in the family provided for a strong and loud rooting section. The boys came to the field with new uniforms in 1922— tan with gray stripes; red and white socks; the players' numbers on the sleeves and "Skillicorn Bros." printed across the front of their jerseys.

Naturally, there had to be substitutes and these included: Tommy Rowan, Stork Novacavich, Dizzy Rubas and Sam Limburgh. The team just played exhibition games in Santa Cruz County though they had several offers to tour the United States but they had good jobs and there wasn't much money in baseball those days. They were the only all-brother team in the United States and, in 1961 their picture was placed in the National Baseball Hall of Fame at Cooperstown, New York. Assemblyman Henry Mello also has one hanging in his office at the State Capitol in Sacramento.

Of the nine brothers, two are still living—Elmer Skillicorn of Watsonville and Eddie Skillicorn in Sacramento. Elmer was the thirteenth child in the family and the youngest on the baseball team.

A game is a game, no matter what the score. But what kind of game is another question. The game of ball on Memorial Day was a "scream" from the girls in the Skillicorn family who were out in force to root for the family, which, of course, was appreciated by them, for they certainly tried hard to get into the lead. Superior playing by the opposite side beat them however. The best they could do was by their champion baserunner, little Elmer, the midget, whose height is about four feet, five inches....

THOMAS ALBRIGHT

Thomas Albright was born in Watsonville in 1876, the son of Joseph and Jane Albright and brother of William, May (Mrs. Frank Tuttle), Josephine (Mrs. George Leland), Myrtle (Mrs. Edward J. Kelly) and Etta. After attending local schools, Tom

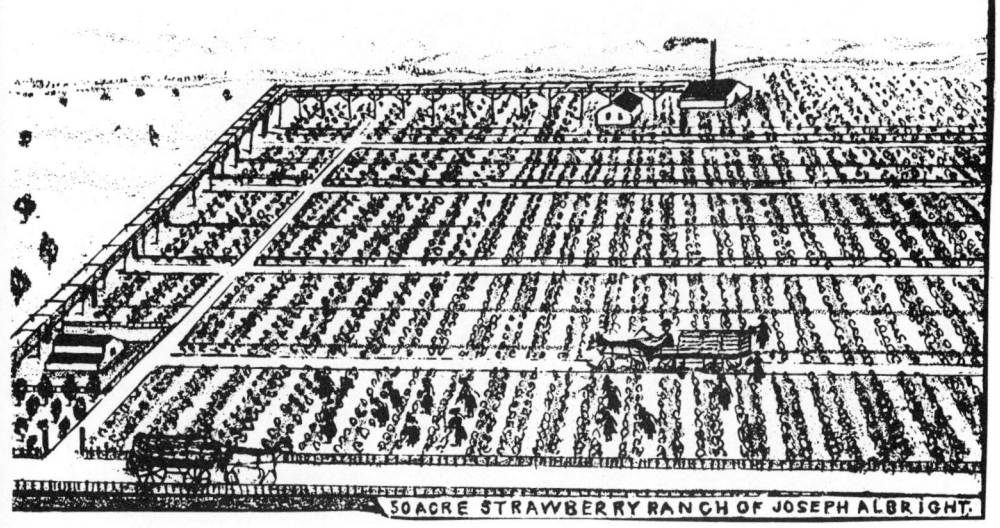

Joseph Albright's fifty-acre strawberry ranch in 1900.

worked on his father's farm for a while and then entered into the blacksmithing business on Main Street. He married Eva Aston in 1900 and they were to have three children. In 1907 Albright ventured into the poltical arena running for the office of police chief—he won the election and was re-elected two years later by a very large majority.

Tom spent many of his leisure hours playing baseball and worked very hard towards establishing a baseball team in Watsonville.

Chief Albright is now wearing the smile that won't wear off, for now over $700 has been subscribed to the local baseball fund and the prospects of raising $1,000 are as bright as the prospects for more rain.
—The *Pajaronian*, 1901

The Three "C" Baseball League was formed that year and Tom became the manager of the local team—the Pippins. Under his leadership the team won the pennant in 1909 and 1910.

Albright was considered a "sure bet" in the 1911 election but the combination of the saloon and church elements made for a "peculiar" election, noted the local paper, and he was ousted by Sylvester Whitsitt for the job of police chief. Albright supported Sunday afternoon baseball, which went against the grain of church goers as well as the saloon trade—bad for business.

Albright became an automobile salesman, being associated with Elmore Lee, who owned the Century Garage. He later sold

Tom Albright, in black suit on the right, was the manager of the Watsonville baseball team.

his interest in the company to H. W. Vaughan and went into business with John Covell, who had the Overland agency. In May of 1916, Albright and another automobile dealer from Santa Cruz, F. A. Shultz, were out on a demonstration ride with Chris Thompson of San Juan Road. After dropping Thompson off at his home, the two men drove toward the Vega railroad crossing where their car was struck by the Del Monte Express and the men were hurled out of the car and killed.

Upon Tom Albright's death at the age of 39, the *Pajaronian* had the following to say:

As a business man he was square, honest and upright, as a friend he was a true companion and a big hearted soul. The death of Mr. Albright has removed one of Watsonville's most popular citizens.

———— • ————

We, the Women's Christian Temperance Union of Watsonville, standing for those principles which uplift humanity tend to a proper observance of the God's Holy Day, do most earnestly deplore and depreciate the appearance of our sister, "The Bloomer Baseball Club," in Watsonville, especially on the sabbath day. Believing that woman's privilege and duty is to elevate and not deteriorate mankind, we wish to plead with all thoughtful fathers and mothers, and all young people to stop and consider what if it were your daughter or your sister, and to use your influence for purity and righteousness on that Holy Day...

—The *Pajaronian*, July 18, 1901

Chapter Four

Let's Go to the Movies

> ... The opposition to the modern motion picture is crumbling and there is a day coming soon when the enemies of the legitimate picture will surrender to the inevitable. Just as every invention of the years past has been born in an environment of distrust and derision and has lived into eternity so will the motion picture come into its own and wear the laurels that it is justly entitled to.
>
> —James Piratsky, editorial, *Evening Pajaronian*, March 30, 1915

Hailed as the newest "novelty" on the American scene, the silent dramas of fact and fancy flickered on the screen in the small and cozy movie houses. These first films were short, one-reelers with subtitles flashed on the screen between scenes. Also on the program would be the vaudeville skit and the ever-present piano player.

The Watsonville Opera House, at 23 East Third (Beach) Street, became known as the Unique Theatre in 1904—five acts of vaudeville and moving pictures for twenty cents admission or ten cents if you sat in the peanut gallery. In 1907 the name was

Built in 1921, the T & D Theatre in Salinas had its formal opening on the first day of November with the musical comedy Angel Face playing to a packed house. This post card was published by the Tubbs Fruit Company, Salinas, in 1922. Shown on the theatre marquee is the name of the film Foolish Wives.

James Piratsky (1850-1949) was the editor of the Evening Pajaronian from 1902 to 1930. He would make the "silents" come alive, standing beside the screen and speaking the various parts, even the villainous villain. His wife managed the La Petite Theatre and the Opera House Theatre.

Billie Burke appeared in person at the T & D Theatre in 1915. She was hailed as "the girl an hour ahead of time."

changed back to the Watsonville Opera House, and that same year John Kersham, well known as a circus ring director throughout California, opened a "palace of amusement" on Main Street.

The Nickelodian, the new electric automatic vaudeville theatre, located at 320 Main Street, opens today and will be continued every day in the week from this date on permanently. During the past year over 150 of these new 5-cent theatres have been opened and are successfully operated ...
—*Evening Pajaronian,* March 23, 1907

In order for Kersham to stay above-board in the theatre business, 6,000 admissions at five cents a head were necessary each month, and since this could not be maintained, he had to close down the Nickelodeon in May and return to the circus world as a trainer of dogs and ponies.

A man by the name of Sumnor Burton came to town in September of 1907 to try his hand at the motion picture business. He was considered one of the most successful managers in the state, having worked with a number of movie houses in southern California. Burton signed a lease agreement with Sol Hildreth for the use of space in the Hildreth Block which was then occupied by the Rendezvous Billiard Parlor. After being vacated, the room was fitted up as a movie house and named the "La Petite Theatre." On the opening night, October 5, people thronged to the new theatre and "scores" were turned away as the overflow crowd from the three performances extended almost to the center of Main Street.

Price of admission to the La Petite was ten cents for adults and five cents for children under ten years of age. The program consisted of such goodies as *Struggle For Life,* a thrilling story of hairbreadth escapes and exciting action, and *Buying a Ladder,* a strong comedy subject full of laughs from start to finish. The price of admission also included illustrated songs sung by Mr. Fred Radone—the ladies hung on his every note!

In January of 1908 Mrs. James Piratsky, wife of the *Evening Pajaronian* editor, bought out Burton's lease and immediately made improvements to the theatre such as a "neat little stage," additional seating, and a new lighting system. When the doors swung open to the public on January 14, included in the price of a ticket were such dramas as *The Clockmaker's Secret*, a tragic story of an old clockmaker who made a compact with the Evil One in order to win the competition for making a clock for his native town. Also shown was a comedy, *The Sailor's Practical Joke*, touted as "one great big roar from its start."

What made these short movies even more appealing was that Jim Piratsky was often on hand to provide the narration and sound effects as he stood alongside the screen. He gathered quite a following with his clever and imaginative performances, and it was said that the drummers would try to schedule their stops in Watsonville when Piratsky was appearing at the theatre, making those silents come alive. But in December of 1909, the La Petite closed down when Mrs. Piratsky and Mr. Hildreth could not come to terms on a new lease agreement.

Not everyone was in favor of this new form of entertainment; at least not on Sundays:

The attempt of the pastors of this city to forever close all theatres and amusements on Sundays was given at least a temporary death blow last night when at the special session of the mayor and board of aldermen it was found that the alleged local ordinance prohibiting theatres running on Sundays and which the pastors demanded shall be enforced, does not exist and that therefore there is no law against the Sunday theatre in this city...

—*Evening Pajaronian*, December 29, 1909

Under new management in January of 1910, the La Petite opened under a new name, the Lyric Theatre. On the program were three reels of moving pictures, a double act of vaudeville, and illustrated songs—still for only ten cents! By 1912, admission was up to fifteen cents per person and included in the price of admission was a one-act play, *To Kill a Man*, a comedy, *His Little Sister*, and Harry James with his latest songs.

Theatres were springing up all over the country as people loved to be entertained and to enter the fascinating world of make-believe. A deep, narrow building was desirable as seats were brought in, and at first a sheet would often be strung up at one end for the screen. The Japanese theatre over in Brooklyn opened in 1910, and that same year Mrs. Piratsky took over the management of the Opera House Theatre, again enlisting her husband to help out.

Alas, with this new film entertainment came the "con" game:

We warn our people against buying any stock in moving picture companies unless they are fully satisfied that the investment is a good one... The public carried away by the enormous profits amassed by the pioneers in the moving picture business are likely to regard with favor any chance given to break into the game. Accordingly, we warn our readers against buying any stock in moving pictures, fake stock companies or from swindlers who represent that they will make rich returns from the "Chain of Theatres." Leave them severely alone or you will dearly repent your gullibility.
—*Evening Pajaronian*, December 15, 1914

An example of this could very easily have been "The Dot," a hurriedly renovated small theatre in the Mansion House block. It opened its doors on the night of February 11, 1913 to "large audiences" and then disappeared from sight as the manager went on to greener pastures. Another theatre that had a relatively short existence in Watsonville was the "New Lyric," which opened on November 30, 1914 in the Brewington Block (now the Kalich Building), 430 Main Street. By January of 1916 it had to close its doors, and the furnishings were sold to the T & D Theatre to help pay some of the outstanding debts.

Not all theatres, naturally, were bad investments or doomed for failure. A case in point was the T & D, a new movie house built in 1915 by the Appleton Investment Company, Otto D. Stoesser, president, Charles Langley, Philip Sheehy, S. Waldo Coleman, John Trafton, F. P. Krough, Frank Rodgers, C. H. Baker, and T. M. Wright. This new theatre was the first building to be erected in Watsonville for just that purpose. Designed by William Weeks, it formally opened to the public on the night of July 2, 1915, with a packed house that saw Billie Burke, touted as "the girl an hour ahead of time," perform in *Jerry*.

When the first strains of the pipe organ swept through the building nearly every seat in the house was occupied. The display of the latest modes in gowns and millinery in all parts of the house gave the opening the appearance of a fashion show and added to the occasion... From the opening number until the falling of the curtain on the last act of the

The flood of 1911. The Lyric Theatre, to the right, opened in 1910 in the Hildreth Block. It was formerly called the La Petite, and later the Pippin. As the Pippin, it closed its doors in 1915.

This advertisement appeared in the newspaper on April 21, 1915.

Left: Charles Chaplin as the employee in "Pay Day."

Below: "Our Gang" appeared at the Appleton Theatre in 1927. Courtesy Sam Stark.

Right: This post card showed scenes from Universal City, "the most wonderful city in the world."

Above: A 1922 post card picture of W. C. Fields.

December 1916 advertisement.

The T & D Theatre became the Appleton, then the State Theatre.

The Fox Theatre in 1926, before the tower was added.

play the audience enjoyed every moment. It was a gala occasion and the patrons of the theatre made the most of their opportunity...
—*Evening Pajaronian*, July 3, 1915

The theatre was leased to Turner and Dahnken of San Francisco for a period of ten years and became known as the T & D Theatre. Theatre goers were pleased with what they saw when entering the movie house:

... The advertising curtain is featured with a striking painting of El Pajaro Springs, the painting being drawn from an actual photograph. There are about two dozen curtains all on the stage, including the flies. The seats throughout the house are covered with leather, the backrests being also of leather. The only difference between the seats in the down stairs portion and those in the balcony and gallery is that the seats down stairs are made more comfortable with springs, those upstairs having no springs...
—*Evening Pajaronian*, June 22, 1915

With the advent of these larger movie houses, the small and cozy little theatres soon closed. The La Petite, renamed the Lyric and the Pippin, passed into oblivion in October of 1915, a few months after the T & D had opened. Though this latter theatre was to have a long run, it was not without its problems, and the major one developed in the form of a newer and larger movie theatre built on the corner of Main and Maple. The year was 1923; gas was selling for eleven cents a gallon, and Prohibition was in full swing. The Zar Saloon stood on that corner next to the Hildreth Building, but, because of Prohibition, the city directory listed the place of business as a "soft drink parlor"! The saloon was moved elsewhere and the lot cleared as construction began on the structure designed by G. Albert Lansburgh. He had been the architect for the Golden Gate Theatre and Loew's Warfield Theatre in San Francisco. This new movie house was built by the El Pajaro Theatre Company headed by Edward Pfingst, leased by the West Coast Theatre Company, and named the California Theatre. It opened on September 19, 1923 with *Steve*, a love thrill in three acts starring Eugene O'Brien. General admission was twenty-seven cents, loges forty-five cents, and children ten cents, with a very "high-class" vaudeville program offered every Sunday. A month after the California Theatre's auspicious opening, the T & D closed down.

This was what might have been expected. The theatre has been run at a loss of from 25 to 30 dollars a day, since the new California Theatre opened, and it was merely a question of how long the lessees would stand such a loss...
—*Evening Pajaronian*, October 22, 1923

In November of 1924 the T & D was gutted by fire with a loss of $50,000 to the Appleton Investment Company. However, repairs were made and soon new life was breathed into the theatre when the Markowitz Brothers of San Francisco leased the T & D and completely refurbished it as the Appleton Theatre, renamed in deference to its owners. A very handsome souvenir booklet was published for the opening night on October 1, 1925. Listed under staff personnel were usherettes Josephine Jones, Anna Hrepich, Anna Felix, Lavisa Johnstone, Edythe Gianotti, Dorita Raymond and Bonita Raymond. Cecil B. De Mille's production *The Coming of Amos*, starring Rod La Rocque, Jetta Goudal and Noah Beery, was the first movie to be shown.

The year 1927 saw the Appleton Theatre "re-opened" again, after being thoroughly renovated. New maroon-colored velour draperies were hung throughout, and new stage scenery was installed, including thirty new drops as settings for the vaudeville acts. Present at the grand opening were the children of

California-Fox Theatre, built in 1923, after remodeling which included the addition of a Spanish tower in 1931. This photograph was taken in 1946.

The Fox Theatre in 1948.

"Our Gang" comedies, who presented a take-off on *Uncle Tom's Cabin*.

That same year, *The Jazz Singer* with Al Jolson made its debut as a "talkie," but it contained only partially spoken dialogue with some subtitles still being used. In January of 1929 the people of Watsonville saw their first all-talking movie at the California Theatre—*Melody of Love* starring Walter Pidgeon. The advertisements read:

Human emotion expressed in dramatic dialogue—the wonder of wonders—talking pictures—hear and see it on the screen—the performance of every member of the unusual cast will delight you—all the characters speak their lines.

—The *Pajaronian*, January 1929

The theatre was packed to the rafters as, many for the first time, people heard the voices of their favorite movie stars. Some turned out to be a distinct disappointment! As to that first "talkie," Ralph Salazar, then a reporter for the *Pajaronian*, noted:

This reporter will not raise hosannas in favor of the talkies, nor will he slash the critters to pieces. Each person can best decide how good or bad are talking pictures...

—The *Pajaronian*, January 1929

But in spite of the drawbacks and mediocre films, people flocked to the movies, those palaces of amusement where you could forget the depression and your cares and be enveloped by the thrilling chase, the "screamingly" funny comedy, or the "edge-of-your-seat" drama on the silver screen.

Changes were still going on in the local movie houses as the California Theatre became the Fox Theatre in 1931, when the Fox West Coast Theatre chain took over the management, as they also did of the Appleton Theatre in 1935, renaming it the State Theatre. In June of 1949, the State, under the management of Robert Lara, began showing a Spanish-speaking film every Tuesday night for the convenience of the Spanish speaking residents of the valley. In 1966, the old T & D, Appleton, and finally the State Theatre closed its doors when the building was purchased by the Charles Ford Company and converted into a warehouse.

There were other theatres in Watsonville, such as the Pajaro Theatre at 255 Main Street which opened in 1925 and eventually

The El Pajaro Theater Company had its checking account at the Pajaro Valley National Bank in Watsonville.

The corner property, the Zar Saloon and a shoe shop, became the site of the California Theatre in 1923, built by the El Pajaro Theater Company (now the Fox Theatre).

was dubbed the "flea house"! The Centre Theatre, first called the Rodeo Theatre, was built in 1948, and the Starlite Drive-In was built in 1949. At one time there was a Japanese Theatre on Bridge Street, near Union, in the school building. A number of theatres were planned, and some were started but not finished:

New Theater To Be Built Here By Fox . . . would erect a building on the corner of Hyde St., Main St. and Western Drive where the Hyde floral shop and warehouse is now located, the cost to be approximately $250,000. In addition to the theatre, the structure will house the Hyde shop and warehouse . . . The new cinema, to be named the "Hyde Park Theatre," will be of the latest design, seating 1200, with no expense spared for comfort and enjoyment of the patron.
—*Register Pajaronian*, January 31, 1946

Excavation began in May of 1947 by the Granite Construction Company, but the project was never completed due to several reasons, including the finding of a natural spring on the property.

Up until World War II as many as ninety million people went to the movies each week in the United States. Television arrived on the scene and people stayed home to watch their favorite situation comedy or old-time movie, causing a decline in attendance at the local movie houses.

Gone are those carefree and glorious days when one could take his favorite girl to the movies for ten or fifteen cents, buy a bag of popcorn for a nickel, then settle down in the seat (hopefully with springs!) and watch such greats as Rin Tin Tin in *Where the North Begins* or the fourteenth episode of *The Reckoning of the Clutching Hand*. Those were the "good old days"!

The new Japanese Theatre in Brooklyn opened last night and the audience that took in the opening bill would make Coxe's army look like the last rose of summer after a beer wagon had gone over it—there was a mob . . . The seating capacity of the new house is about 400 but there were 500 Japanese there, if not more. As for the play that was being given, the two reporters present almost threw a fit trying to figure out just who the villain was and who was the leading man . . . The show opened up shortly after dark and closed at twelve o'clock. This evening the play will be "The Pajama Kid or Who Swiped the Mikado's Overalls?"
—*Evening Pajaronian*, January 4, 1910

Pajaro School in the 1890s. Miss Grimes was the teacher.

Eureka School. The district was organized in 1884. In 1946 it was annexed to Corralitos.

Chapter Five

The Small Schoolhouse

Out on Green Valley Road at number 1737 stands a dwelling owned by Angelino Mello that was once used for a schoolhouse called Ferndale because of the many ferns in the surrounding area. The school was built in 1908 on land donated by Joseph and Maria Tavares. The first teacher in the eight-grade school was Blossom Staples, who roomed and boarded at a nearby farmhouse as did many country teachers in those early days. In order to raise money to buy equipment for the school, the children would gather prunes from the trees in the school yard and Grandma Tavares would dip the fruit in lye, dry it, and package it for selling.

The motto of the school was "Our School In the Heart of the Hills" and it served that mountain area for thirty-eight years, until 1946, when the school was closed down and the children were sent to other schools. Ferndale School was converted into a residence in 1949 and is now used by farmworkers on the Mello property.

——— • ———

In 1862 a new school district called Lindley was established over on the Monterey side of the Pajaro River. A schoolhouse was built, and in 1876 a concerned citizen of Watsonville visited the school and reported the following: "I spent an hour a few days since in visiting the Lindley School near the Pajaro depot, in charge of Mr. and Mrs. Underwood. The building has been recently moved to the west side of the road and well furnished with maps, charts, black boards and improved desks, still it is too small and entirely unsuited for school purposes. The district is one of the most wealthy in the county and the citizens should have pride and public spirit enough to induce them to provide a better school building."

In 1887, eleven years after this article appeared in the *Pajaronian*, a new schoolhouse was built, designed by Alex Chalmers of Watsonville. The William Volck Museum of Watsonville has in its files an invitation to the Lindley School graduation in 1901, which was held at the Guild Hall in Watsonville.

Some of the students who attended this school back before the turn of the century were William McGowan, Annie Cox, Jerry Sheehy, Julia Horgan, Ethel Allison, Andrew Dethlefsen and Horace White.

———— • ————

Driving out Green Valley Road and turning into number 315, you would see a building in back of the main house which is being used as a day nursery. This structure was once the Amesti School. The school district had been formed in 1879 and an earlier school building was constructed in 1881 at a cost of $285, with J. C. Aston the contractor. In 1913 a new schoolhouse was built, the one still standing, which was designed by H. B. Douglas; J. H. W. Jones was the contractor. The building measured thirty-eight by forty-two feet and contained one large schoolroom, library, teacher's rest room, lockers, and a girls' dressing room. The heating was provided by a double jacket stove, and the new school boasted of many other "modern" conveniences. On the school board were Martin Bonde, James Holohan and Herbert Cowles. An addition was made to the school in 1924 by contractors T. N. and H. N. Alford. A new school building was constructed on Amesti Road in 1946 and the old school and property were sold to Lynden Forrester, who built a home on the front portion of the property. The two buildings are now owned by the Cadwalader family.

On the first Monday of August 1868, the County Board of

Supervisors created the Green Valley School District by dividing the Oak Grove District into two parts—Corralitos and Green Valley. On August 13 a meeting was held at the home of a Mr. Ketchum for the purpose of deciding on whether or not to build a new school house. James Cathers donated one acre of land atop a small hill and the Green Valley School was built. It measured thirty by twenty-four feet, and the first teacher was W. H. Hobbs. In 1898 a special tax was levied on Green Valley property owners of seventy cents on every one hundred dollars to build another schoolhouse replacing the old one that had burned down. W. H. Weeks was the architect for the new building and A. D. Cloud of San Jose the contractor. His was the lowest bid at $994. The teacher at the new schoolhouse was C. Keith Hill, who was replaced by Maud Jones in 1899. When the Salsipuedes School District was formed in 1946, the Green Valley school was closed down and eventually converted into a residence. It is now the home of Bert and Kay Spencer.

——— • ———

The Carrolton School District was formed in 1861 and named after the first teacher in the valley, Seneca Carroll. Those first students learned their ABC's in a small building located near Thompson's corner on San Juan Road. By 1868 it was decided to build a new schoolhouse nearer the center of the district, and D. M. Clough donated land for this purpose, also on San Juan Road. When the "iron horse" made its way to the Pajaro Valley in 1871, it passed right behind the schoolhouse and created a fascinating diversion for the youngsters.

Some of the students were older boys who were sometimes hard to control, and one teacher, H. F. Courter, started off his term by showing how adept he was with a gun. He then laid it on his desk and told his pupils he expected discipline in the classroom. He got it!

The Carrolton School has closed for the winter and the efficient teacher, J. H. McEven, will soon go to Sumner to resume charge of the school he had last winter.

—November 27, 1879

Calabasas school children, 1915.

Carrolton School about 1901. The teacher is Miss Sarah Nicholson and the students are Shirley Rowe, Leroy Beilby, Ellen Frondsen, Lizzie Hoyt, May Carey, Walter Eaton, Willie Rowe, Charley Eaton, Lemmie Carey, Eddie Frondsen, Claude Beilby, Gladys Mann, Bessie Eaton, and Hazel Eaton.

The Larkin Valley School District was organized in 1875. This building, shown as it looked in the 1930s, was built in 1916. It is now a private residence.

Roache School on February 11, 1904. The teachers were Margaret Sparks and Edna Cutler. The building was constructed in 1903, William Weeks, architect.

School for Aromas, built in 1895, designed by William Weeks. A new schoolhouse was built in 1925, preceding the present one.

Last day of school in the Hazel Dell District, about 1890. Second from the right in the top row is Clara Johnson Leask, the teacher. Directly below her is Mary Joseph. The gentleman in the picture is Frank Joseph, Mary's father, trustee of the district. Next to him is Mrs. Fannie Johnson, the mother of the teacher.

In 1880 the school report showed that in July there had been seventy-three pupils attending Carrolton School. Honor students were Johanna Clough, Julia Kerr, Bella Cassin, Willie Stow, Maggie Thompson, Julia Clough, Maggie Speegle, Elmer Snyder, and Jennie Marcus. The school burned down in 1935.

——— • ———

The new school building in the Railroad District being erected by John Aston, is almost completed and will be ready for occupancy soon after the 1st of September.
—The *Pajaronian*, August 28, 1878

Started in 1869, the Railroad School was so named because talk was rampant about the railroad's coming to Watsonville and it was first thought the tracks would be laid north of the Pajaro River, but it was not to be. This area, about two miles out of Watsonville on Riverside Road, was the site of the new school in 1878. In 1890 it was the first school in the valley to fly the American flag. The ceremonies were held on April 18, just sixteen years to the day before the "big" quake.

By 1899 the school building was too small and architect Weeks designed a new structure which was built on property donated by the Kelly-Thompson family. The old school was sold to the Silliman family in 1900 and still stands on the Silliman ranch. In 1900, when Miss Louise Kidder was the teacher, those on the honor roll were Edna Mann, Kate Coward, Edith Mann, Kate Howard, Maggie Coward, Carl Silliman, Kitty Thompson, Alice Silliman, Russell Thompson, Frank Reagan, and Raymond Driscoll.

The Railroad School was annexed to Salsipuedes in 1946 and that second school building was torn down and the property reverted back to the Kelly-Thompson family.

——— • ———

In 1879 the Beach Road School was built on the Ring property and a few of the family names of the children who attended classes were Thurwachter, Richardson, Knowles, Foster, Silva, King, Lewis, Bridgewater, and Souza. Louise Thurwachter, better known as Lou, returned to the school in 1894 as a teacher. Two years earlier the school had been closed down due to a lack of pupils (there were only five), but attendance picked up and the school was re-opened. Miss Thurwachter resigned from her position in 1904 to become the wife of Henry Schroeder, much to the dismay of her pupils, who liked her very much.

The new teacher was Miss Onie Ross and she received the magnificent salary of fifty dollars a month. The small schoolhouse was sold in 1909 to James Redman for forty dollars, and he had the building moved to his property. A new schoolhouse was built, designed by William Weeks, and it stood out on Beach Road until 1929 when the building, no longer used as a school, was sold to the Springfield School District, Monterey County, for $500 and was moved over to the Salinas Road replacing one that had burned down.

This schoolhouse was sold to a private party in 1972 and restored for commercial use, and still sits atop the hill overlooking the road from Watsonville to Moss Landing, next to the present school. The first Beach Road school, on the Redman property, was torn down in 1937 and the lumber was used in building a shed.

———— • ————

In the 1800s there were a number of private schools in Watsonville, and one such institution was the Grace School founded in 1870 at the northeast corner of Lincoln and East Beach streets, on Blackburn property. This was a day school where the primary and academic branches of learning were taught under the leadership of the Rev. D. O. Kelley. Terms, per month, were four dollars for pupils under ten years of age; five dollars for students ten to fifteen years; and six dollars for those over fifteen years of age. In 1875 a Mrs. M. P. Southworth and Mrs. Fannie McGhee, former teachers at the Memphis Ladies Institute, took over the Grace School. The Rev. Kelley remained to teach Latin and bookkeeping. But, three years later, in 1878, the school closed down and the ladies left the community due to ill health.

The local paper noted: "In Mrs. Southworth's room the progress made by the younger pupils during the past three years was wonderful. Looking into the bright faces of the score of boys and girls in the class, we could easily believe the teachers' proud statement that there was not a sly or deceitful one among them."

For sale, $2,500, school property corner Third and Lincoln streets. Two large school houses and a large well furnished dwelling house. Size of lot 290 ft. by 260 ft.—an improved portion of this lot 290 by 160 ft. will be sold for $500.

—The *Pajaronian*, March 30, 1882

Professor P. K. Dibble opened a private high school in one of these old school buildings in April of 1882. The building had formerly been used by Professor William Van Doren, who had also run a private school.

A Blackburn house on East Beach was gutted by fire in 1903 and the newspaper stated that the house had formerly been a private school, but which one is still unknown.

The graduating class of *Pleasant Valley* or *Hungry Hollow School* (year unknown), left to right, Gilbert Cox, Alice Reid, Leslie Cox, Mary Sylva, and Willie Wilson.

THIS AND THAT

In 1864 the school census showed that there were 140 boys attending school in Watsonville between the ages of four and eighteen, and 306 girls. Thirty-nine were attending private school. There were ten Negro children and two Indian children.

———   •   ———

There is one common practice which ought to be abolished in our public schools at once, and everywhere without question or parley. That is the practice of imprisoning the children in the school houses beyond school hours. Pretty nearly every school house in the land is thus turned into a penitentiary in which children are immured every day, some of them for imperfect recitations, others for fault of deportment...
—The *Pajaroninan*, April 29, 1880

———   •   ———

The following is from a Santa Cruz County booklet published in 1914 listing the teachers and prinicpals (if any) in the Pajaro Valley country schools:

Amesti	Edna E. Anderson, teacher
Browns' Valley	Mrs. Flora B. Tupper, teacher
Calabasas	Bernice McLellan, teacher
Carlton	Styleta C. Kane, teacher
Casserly	Marie O. Rowe, principal
	Ella A. Martin, teacher
Corralitos	Anna Paulsen, principal
	Ruth Rodgers, teacher
	Helen Brassel, teacher
Eureka	Lena Schafer, teacher
Ferndale	Florence Harris, teacher
Fruitvale	Mary E. Caddy, teacher
Green Valley	Margaret S. Algar, teacher
Hazel Dell	Ranghild Frykland, teacher
Hill	Edna Rowe, teacher
Las Manzanitas	Mrs. Mary W. Avancina, teacher
Railroad	Mrs. Ouida Rudasill, teacher
Redwood	Eula Craighead, teacher
Roach(e)	Mrs. Mary Y. Tyler, teacher
San Andreas	Marjorie March, teacher

Chapter Six

Houses and Moving Day

MORRIS TUTTLE HOME

All branches of work in connection with construction and furnishing of M. B. Tuttle's handsome new home on Lake Avenue have been completed, and Mr. Tuttle and family are now occupying it. They have a home in which they can take pardonable pride, and which is one of the most finished and complete residences in this county or near-by districts...
—The *Pajaronian*, January 18, 1900

Eighteen ninety-nine saw a building boom in the town of Watsonville as houses and blocks of buildings sprang up like mushrooms and the city's boundaries were pushed even further out. Architect William H. Weeks, who lived in Watsonville at the time, was responsible for many of the new structures, including the Lewis Block, Railroad School, Moreland Notre Dame Academy, and Stoesser Building on West Third. Residences to his credit, either new or remodeled, were done for A. N. Judd, Kelly-Thompson, George Martin, John T. Porter, Dr. P. K. Watters, L. V. Willets, Warren Porter, and last but not least, Morris Tuttle, whose new home was at 723 East Lake Avenue. All of these homes were either finished or under construction in 1899.

Tuttle had commissioned Weeks to draw plans for his new

The Morris Tuttle home as it looked in the 1920s.

home back in the winter of 1898, and construction began in the spring of 1899. Bids for the carpentry work on the house were opened in March, with B. F. Owsley of San Jose the lowest bidder at $5,147. The hardwood finish for the interior was provided by the Santa Clara Mill and Lumber Company at $2,500, and other contracts were let to A. P. Beck, plumbing; F. R. Bradbury, painting; W. A. White, electric wiring; and the Charles Ford Company, furnishings.

William H. Weeks

The woodwork for the interior of M. B. Tuttle's Lake Avenue residence is from the Loma Prieta mill in this city. It turns out work equal to that of any mill in the State.

—The *Pajaronian*, August 31, 1899

By the end of the year the large and commodious house was receiving its finishing touches and the magnificent structure provided the passer-by with quite a sight—the rounded porch with its stone pedestals and strange gargoyles; the circular tower; the balcony; and many ornamentations around the plate glass windows. As one entered the house past the mahogany door and the leaded, beveled windows, the beautiful inlaid oak floor of the entry hall caught the attention. To the right was the parlor whose

This home for William Grul was built in 1898 at 33 Brennan Street. W. H. Weeks was the architect. The house was later moved up the hill to 108 High Street.

walls were finished in rare crotch mahogany. The mantle over the fireplace was of special design by architect Weeks, and the inlaid floor boasted both oak and rosewood.

Other rooms on the lower floor were a bedroom, living room, dining room, library, lavatory, kitchen, servants' room, pantry, and porch. In the kitchen were speaking tubes which connected with the upper floor, and in the dining room one could summon the servants by pushing the electric bell. Up on the second floor were six bedrooms finished in white cedar, pine, and birdseye maple. There were also a lavatory and bathroom plus medicine and linen closets.

The attic has been floored over and is being used as one large room. It is a playroom for the children on unpleasant days and a billiard table with complete equipment shows that the head of the family finds it a place for recreation...

—The *Pajaronian*, January 18, 1900

And how about the head of the family, the man who had this beautiful home built for his family, and for a place to entertain his

The Ingham house was remodeled in 1896 by architect Weeks. In 1925 it was moved from 517 Main Street to 22 High Street.

business associates and friends? Morris Burns Tuttle was born in Iowa in 1858, one of nine children born to Owen and Mary Tuttle. The family came to the Pajaro Valley in 1872 by train, just one year after the Southern Pacific had laid track from Gilroy through the Chittenden Pass area and into Pajaro across the river. A brother of Owen, Daniel Tuttle, met his relatives at the station and they all bundled into a hay wagon and made their way to Daniel's ranch out in the Beach Road district, near the river. Soon afterwards Owen purchased land on East Lake Avenue and moved his family into a new home.

Morris, along with his brothers and sisters, attended local schools and was to become very knowledgeable on farming and horticulture. In 1878, at the age of twenty, he went over to Hollister where he managed a farm owned by his father. In 1880 he married a Hollister girl by the name of Mary Ingles. The young couple moved back to Watsonville several years later and lived in a small home further out on East Lake Avenue than the present house. Tuttle became the owner of 300 acres and raised apples and hops.

M. B. Tuttle has put in a horse-power pumping plant at his farm on the Salsipuedes Creek and is irrigating his hop yard. The pump is running day and night, and is intended to give the yard a good soaking. This is a new departure in the hop business in the Pajaro Valley.
—The *Pajaronian*, April 26, 1894

Morris and Mary Tuttle were the parents of Warren, Lee, Owen, Mabel, Gladys, and Adele. Mary Ingles Tuttle died in 1926; Morris Tuttle died in 1937; and the last of their children, Gladys Tuttle McSherry, died last year (1979). At Morris's death the local paper noted:

Morris Tuttle grew up here, watching the progress and development of a thriving community. He raised hops in the early days and was one of the first orchardists here. Mr. Tuttle was also for many years director of the old Bank of Watsonville...
—*Register-Pajaronian*, September 30, 1937

His son, Warren Tuttle, inherited the house and, in 1939, hired architect Ralph Wyckoff to draw plans for the remodeling of the interior of the structure, making it into four "modern" apartments with a kitchen and garage for each tenant. Prior to this the house had been used by Dr. A. Ray Lawn, local chiropractor and diet specialist, as a "health home."

The Tuttle house was to change owners several times after going out of the hands of the Tuttle family, and in 1974 it was purchased by the present owners, Oliver Realty and Oliver and Campos Builders, with the interior being remodeled into office suites.

This large and stately structure graces the eastern entrance into Watsonville, providing a gentle but obvious reminder of the city's past and the wealth that some of our hardy pioneers gleaned from the valley's fertile soil.

MAPLE AVENUE

In March of 1865, Joseph Ordish opened a street through his property which he named Maple Avenue, having planted 250 maple trees along the new thoroughfare. But it wasn't until 1888 that Hawkins and Peckham purchased the property between Union and Marchant and sold off lots at $325 each. The Spreckels Sugar Plant was being constructed in Watsonville and more

Maple Avenue in 1905.

homesites were needed for the workers. This new tract helped to fill the void.

The 100 block has long been a street of lovely old homes, large and small, and the two at numbers 144 and 148 are fine examples of cottages built here before the turn of the century. They were designed and built by Joseph Aston in 1892, one for William Trafton, who later became mayor of the town, and the other for a local businessman by the name of T. C. Pierson.

Across the street at number 139 is a pink and white house built in 1890 for T. J. Horgan, fruit and produce broker. A reporter from the *Pajaronian* visited the house just before the final touches were put on, and wrote the following:

The front door is mainly of cathedral glass. To the right of the hall is the parlor with a bay window facing Maple Avenue. Folding doors separate the parlor form the dining room. The folding doors are paneled in curly and burl redwood, and the dark finish of the former and light finish of the latter, bring out all the beauties of these fine specimens of redwood, and combined make very artistic doors. A feature of the dining room is the massive and beautiful mantle in Spanish cedar that rests above the tiled fireplace . . .

The reporter goes on to say that there were three bedrooms, a bathroom, kitchen, and pantry, each room supplied with gas fixtures.

At number 110 the property was purchased in 1893 by Mateo Lettunich for $650 and, in 1895 he hired William Weeks to draw plans for a two-story Queen Anne style house. The contractor was M. J. Downey, and the house was built at a cost of $3,900. The house next door, at number 114, was also a Lettunich house designed by Weeks, but of a different architectural style. The house was rented out to the Osborn family for many years.

On the corner of Maple and Marchant at number 163 stands a two-story house built in 1900 for Mrs. Israel Johnson, better known as Mam-Mam Johnson, the mother of Mrs. Samuel Leask of Santa Cruz. The two-story blue and white house at number 135 was built for James Sheehy, fruit broker, in 1893.

Contractor Aston is rushing work on the new houses of James Sheehy on Maple Avenue. There are only five vacant lots on Maple Avenue and it is stated that A. Newman will soon build one of them.
—The *Pajaronian*, March 30, 1893

There have been some changes on Maple Avenue over the years—old houses being torn down and new ones going up—but there are a lot of those original homes still standing as a reminder of our city's rich architectural heritage.

——— • ———

Many homes in Watsonville were moved from the downtown area to make room for the growing business section, thus saving a lot of houses from the wrecking ball.

I the undersigned, am prepared to do all kinds of house moving and raising and carpenter work for $3 per day. Ten hours for a days work. The Public is howling for low wages. Now is the time to do your moving. Watsonville is with the railroads, I will have it with the carpenters and house movers.

(signed) Felix Grundy Gaddie
—The *Pajaronian*, April 24, 1886

H. P. Brassel had a home built for himself and his family in 1880 at 21 West Lake Avenue. This house now stands at 200 Marchant Street. The two houses next door were also moved, from the southeast corner of Lincoln and East Lake to their present Marchant Street location. Old-timers call them the "sisters."

The James Ingham home stood at 517 Main Street and was

The residence of Geo. P. Martin was built in 1899 at 309 East Lake Avenue. It was later moved to 59 Airport Road.

The former home of Frank Rider at Fifth and Lincoln was moved in 1910 to 202 East Beach Street. Now apartments, it is owned by Mr. and Mrs. D'Arcy Bonnet. The man wearing an apron is A. A. Krogh.

remodeled by architect Weeks in 1896. This structure was moved in 1925 up to 22 High Street and is now the home of Jim and Georgia Miller. One of the longest moves was that of the George Martin home, built in 1899 at 309 East Lake. It was moved up to 59 Airport Road and still stands there today.

In 1884 Charles Ford had four cottages built behind his store on West Beach Street. When the Appleton Hotel was built in 1911, these structures were moved to various parts of town. Two are standing on White Street near the Pajaro River.

———— • ————

One of the most qualified house movers after the turn of the century was one John Ostrander, whose equipment was housed on East Lake Avenue in back of where the Christian Church now stands. Mr. Ostrander was much in demand in other towns as well and his expertise may be one reason why Watsonville was able to save these structures. The moving operation would often take weeks and involved the use of the caston with a drum in the center, cables, wooden rollers with planks, and horses. In later years, Clark and Clark provided rigging and equipment for moving houses. Their business was located at 250 First Street. In 1954 they moved six houses from Alexander Street to various other locations. One was moved over the Pajaro Bridge onto Bishop Street. Two years ago this house was moved to Riverside Road.

Pleasant Homes—A praiseworthy and cheering feature of the beautiful valley of the Pajaro and contiguous country is the rapid improvements being made in the numerous homes thickly scattered over valley and highlands. Rapid and important changes for the better are going on, more taste is being displayed in the construction of residences, out-buildings, etc., and fences are put up in a more substantial manner with more regard to the surveyor's lines. . . . Some of the finest residences in the county are to be found outside of town limits and neat and ornamental fences enclose front yards which have been made more beautiful with evergreens and rare exotics. Pleasant surroundings have their influence for good in the family circle and happy firesides ever hold the hearts of the sons and daughters who leave the old homestead and frequently brings them back out of the whirl and toil of everyday life."

—The *Pajaronian*, January 25, 1872

Chapter Seven

Fruit Packing Houses

PACKING HOUSES, VINEGAR WORKS AND SHIPPERS

The fruit packing houses in Watsonville sprang up like mushrooms after the turn of the century—Walker Street and the nearby area had become the apple men's mecca. As to the actual operation of the business, thirty to forty men were employed to pick and haul the apples in large boxes to the packing house. The apples were then given to the sorters, about a dozen women who carefully went over the apples and took out the culls. Next in line were the packers who sat on low stools with the apples on one side and the squares of wrapping paper on the other. About sixty boxes of apples were packed a day.

In September of 1903, the ladies walked off the job as they had been promised wages of one dollar for a nine-hour work day and some packers were only paying one dollar for a ten-hour work day. The strike was soon settled to the ladies' satisfaction. At the Simpson and Hack packing plant, the Chinese packers walked off the job because they were not allowed to smoke while working. The plant manager stated that the white man was not allowed to smoke so neither could the Chinese.

——— • ———

One of the first apple packing sheds to be built in Watsonville was that for M. N. and Mateo Lettunich in 1895, located near the

Packing apples at the San Monte Fruit Company.

Watsonville depot on Walker Street. In 1900 the Lettunich company employed several girls to grade apples, and the newspaper noted: "It is a branch of work at which girls excel, and if apples are perfectly graded to start with the pack is apt to be all right." Disaster struck in May of 1903 when three large packing houses were burned to the ground, including the Lettunich's. These fires were said to be of incendiary origin. The small four-inch water mains were insufficient to put out the flames, but M. N. Lettunich was able to save four newly painted fruit wagons.

Work was soon underway to rebuild the packing sheds and the Dewey Brand wrapper was soon being placed on the top grade apples. On extra fancy stock for export, the top layer of fruit was sprinkled with gold and silver gilt, making for a very attractive box. In 1900 the Lettunich company handled about 100,000 boxes of apples and shipped 110 cars of fruit to local and eastern points.

───── • ─────

Chong Wo, a Brooklyn merchant, is going to be in the apple handling business this year. He has been buying by the box and has about ten

MacDonald & Sons, fruit packers, at Walker and Kearney in 1910.

carloads contracted for. This is the first appearance of a Chinaman in the business of buying apples in the Pajaro Valley. He expects to ship to Asiatic ports.

—The *Pajaronian*, 1899

Mr. Wo built a packing and shipping shed over across the river in Pajaro. By 1901 his fruit growing operation was confined to the cultivation of a twenty-acre orchard of decidious fruits and seven acres of strawberries. He employed a large number of workers in his plant and gave his personal attention to the grading of apples, thus insuring an excellent pack. During the season of 1900 he shipped sixty carloads of apples and never received any complaints—the fruit was true to its label and the pack was one of the finest on the market.

———— • ————

By 1906 there were twenty-seven fruit packers and shippers listed in the Watsonville City Directory, and in 1908 six more sheds were being built, made necessary by the great increase in the number of young orchards coming into stronger bearing. The

Hattie George and Irene Hopkins in the office of the Earl Fruit Company, 1911. Courtesy Barbara Hopkins Davis.

packing houses, driers, canneries, and vinegar works now numbered over forty. One of these driers was located on the west side of Walker Street south of Riverside Drive. Built in 1906, it was the largest drier in the valley and contained six large brick furnaces to dry the culls and windfalls. The driers, mostly owned and operated by the Chinese, first used wood for the furnaces—tan oak was hauled down from the hills, the bark was stripped and sent over the the Santa Cruz tannery, while the wood was used locally. When the driers converted to oil, it was purchased from the Watsonville Oil Company, whose oil fields were located out in the Chittenden Pass area—300 barrels a week. The apples would be cut, peeled and sliced, then laid on racks to dry above the furnaces. They were then packed and shipped in fifty-five-pound white pine boxes.

The San Monte Fruit Company was incorporated in 1903 and a large packing house was built near the railroad depot off Walker Street. In 1906 a new packing house was constructed on a four-acre lot at the northwest corner of Walker and First streets. This new building was designed by architect William Weeks and was the largest packing house in the Pajaro Valley at that time. By 1912, San Monte's various plants—cider, vinegar works, drier and fruit packing—were running full blast.

Just a few years before, all the apple peelings and parings from the driers and canneries were dumped into the river, but now these were turned into high grade vinegar. This arm of the mother company was called the Kreiger Vinegar Company and was established in 1908. By 1916 the storage capacity was more than one million gallons.

The apple packing plant, when running at full capacity, shipped from 250 to 300 carloads per season under such brand names as "Quality First," "Sunblest," and "Red Anchor." The San Monte Fruit Company went out of business in the 1920s.

———•———

In the 1910 Watsonville City Directory the following fruit packers and shippers were listed:

FRUIT PACKERS
Alaga Brothers	32 Alexander
Andrishevich and Vucicevich	86 Brennan
Battinich Co.	Walker near Ford
Braycovich, J. P. & Co.	255 Ford
California Fruit Packing Co.	W. Third opposite Pine
Capitanich, J. C.	141 Main
Copeland, J. D.	S.W. corner Walker and Fifth
Copriviza & Gera	Corner Second and Walker
Earl Fruit Co.	W. Third and Walker
Eiggia, John	208 Ford
Gospodnetich, Kosmos	15 Kearney
Grizich, Matthew	570 Main
Gukan, Peter & Co.	706 Rodriguez
Gurash & Stolich	Corner W. Third and Locust
Ivoncouich, Vojvodich & Co.	215 Ford
Kray, John & Co.	217 Ford
Kukuliza, M. & Co.	30 Kearney

The building housing Simpson & Hack Fruit Company was designed by W. H. Weeks, architect. It was built in 1903 at First and Walker streets.

Lettunich, E. B.	146 W. Lake
Lettunich, M. N. & Co.	Corner W. Third and Pine
Loma Fruit Co.	West side Walker between Second and Third
Lucich & Gordon	Union opposite Elm
Martin Bros.	Corner Walker and First
McDonald & Sons	W. Third west of Walker
Mengol, Peter	W. Third and west of Walker
Miljanich, J. & Co.	60 Sixth
Miovich, J. P. & Co.	Corner West Third and Locust
Morse, Milton J.	130 W. Lake
Novacovich & Stolich	514 Walker
Pacific Evaporating Co.	Corner Walker and First
Pajaro Packing Co.	Corner Walker and First
Pecarovich, M. & Co.	148 Fifth
Pekoch, S. & Co.	237 Walker
Perry & Hrepich	234 Walker

Pista, J. & Co.	Martins Court
Pulich, L. & Co.	N.W. corner Ford and Walker
Radovan, Frank	245 Walker
Resetar, Balich & Co.	34 W. Lake Ave.
Rilovich & Co.	159 W. Lake Ave.
Rodonich, N. & Co.	56 Sixth
San Monte Fruit Co.	Corner Walker and First
Sassilo Bros.	704 Walker
Scurich, A. A. & Co.	W. Third opposite Pine
Scurich Bros.	22 Kearney
Scurich, J. & Co.	625 Walker
Secondo Bros.	44 Rodriguez
Simpson, Frank Fruit Co.	Corner Walker and First
Simunovich, Jasper	56 Kearney
Stolich Bros.	162 Fifth
Travers, M. A. Co.	40 Rodriguez
United Apple Growers	N.E. corner Walker and Second
Vlasich, P. & Co.	127 Rodriguez
Windcrest Ranch Co.	122 Rodriguez
Zar Bros.	123 Callahan

FRUIT DRYERS

Chong Tong Kee	N.W. corner E. Third and Beck Ave.

This building originally housed the Watsonville Cider & Vinegar works, which was purchased by Jones Bros. in 1914. They went bankrupt in 1926 and the company was purchased by the Pajaro Valley Vinegar Company. In 1927 the Monarch Vinegar Company took over the plant. The building is now the home of the Speas Company, a subsidiary of Pillsbury.

Hop Chan Apple Evaporating Co.	131 First
Ming, Jan	114 Union
Pacific Evaporating Co.	46 Main
Pajaro Packing Co.	Corner Walker and First
Quong Sung Lung Co.	West side Walker south of First
Wing Sung Lung Co.	Beach Road west end Third

FRUIT CANNERS

Pajaro Packing Co.	Corner Walker and First
Watsonville Canning Co.	18-20 Menker

VINEGAR MANUFACTURERS

Jones Bros. & Co.	12 Menker
Krieger Vinegar Co.	Corner Walker and First

——— • ———

On a balmy Saturday afternoon in June of 1915, more than one thousand men and women gathered together in the Second Street auditorium to organize the Watsonville Apple Distributors. This newly founded organization was to help perfect the packing, shipping and marketing of apples from Watsonville. Attorney John Gardner was the presiding officer and Carroll Rodgers the secretary at this mass meeting. Others on the thirteen-man committee were: W. R. Radcliff, C. H. Baker, Geo. Copriviza, W. J. McGrath, H. M. Tenny, J. W. Baxter, C. F. Langley, F. S. Jerome, J. B. Cutter, J. W. Tullock, Edward White and M. N. Lettunich. A membership list of the newly formed organization was printed in the newspaper in July of 1915—five brokers, fifteen commercial packers, 150 growers and 180 merchants, business and professional men. Indeed, the apple industry was at its peak and, as that 1915 report noted, for the first time in the history of the apple business, the bankers and business men, generally, had come to the realization that to them the success of the apple industry in this valley was vital.

——— • ———

In 1928 the first commercial apple washer made in the valley appeared in the industry. This machine was made by Everett Goodale, and its construction and first use took place on a small ranch on the Riverside road. Today, this type of washing equipment is used in apple packing plants throughout the region. Years ago the fruit was placed in crates and merely hand-dipped in barrels or tanks. Then, later, a somewhat more expedient and less laborious method was devised where the fruit was dipped in partitioned troughs, one-half containing the acid or cleaning solution and the other half the rinse water. This commercial washer that was invented by Goodale did away with the method just described and sped up the process. The first washer, made in 1928, was not placed on the market for commercial use until 1931. Since then there have been about one hundred manufactured and assembled on Menker Street. The size of the washer varies anywhere from a 100-box to a 400-box an hour capacity machine. A washer of this type weighs anywhere from 800 pounds to two tons. All of the woodwork and assemblying is done in this plant while the metal parts of the machine are manufactured in a local metal shop. It takes four men about five days to make one of these commercial washers.

—*Watsonville Morning Sun*, October 26, 1939

The Corralitos Fruit Growers Association have begun the construction of a dehydrating plant adjoining their packing plant on the Kearney Street extension. The building will be absolutely fireproof with a foundation of brick, a cement floor and the sidewalls will be of a hollow tile with a brick lining and an airspace between. The building and plant completed will cost about $20,000. The Union Construction Company, of San Francisco, has the contract for the erection of the building ... The plant is expected to be completed and ready for operation by the first of July.

—*Evening Pajaronian*, May 14, 1920

This picture was taken in front of Pena and Hall's Clothing Store in the Cooper Block early in this century. In the Buick, left to right, are Charles Boin, Tony Vyeda, Charles Sibole, and Charles Cottrell.

1910 Stearns car which belonged to Elmore Lee, 128 East Beech Street.

Chapter Eight

Horseless Carriages

Now comes the automobile, which claims the attention of roadbuilders. This style of vehicle is rapidly coming into general use for business and pleasure and each owner of such a machine becomes at once an advocate of better roads. Thus does the popular demand for improved highways increase and the good work goes steadily on. In this particular Santa Cruz County is well to the front and is going forward at no uncertain pace. The cutting down of the Green Valley school house hill and other minor improvements outlined by Supervisor Linscott are commendable steps along progressive lines, but the greatest improvement of them all will be the opening up of the road along the Pajaro river below the Chittenden grade to connect Santa Cruz and San Benito counties at a point near Chittenden station. This highway will be practically level and will reduce the distance between Watsonville and Hollister by three miles.

—The *Pajaronian*, September 3, 1903

In 1902, when ping-pong was sweeping the country and "In the Good Old Summer Time" was a hit song, local man "Speed" Miller was trying to work up an automobile craze along Main

Street in Watsonville. The town was without an automobile but a number of men were showing symptoms of the fever. The first to succumb, according to the local newspaper, was Charles Mackrell, a harness maker by profession.

Charles Mackrell received a large and handsome Oldsmobile Tuesday, and is prepared to give sight-seeing parties a delightful spin about the valley and to surrounding towns at reasonable rates.

—The *Pajaronian*, October 2, 1902

This new-fangled mode of transportation made little impression on most of the townspeople—it was thought to be a passing fancy. The horse and carriage were good enough, along with the bicycle, as a means of transportation, and the new "horseless carriage" was merely a curiosity. Back in 1896, one had been featured in the New York Barnum and Bailey circus parade as an "oddity." Those first automobiles before 1900 were handmade to order for only the affluent. The average citizen couldn't afford one and didn't really understand them anyway, nor had most of them ever seen one.

Montgomery Ward purchased two cars at a price of $30,000 each and had them shipped around the United States, stopping off at small towns for people to see and examine. In 1902 there were 8,000 cars made in the United States and Charles Mackrell's curved-dash Oldsmobile was one of the first successful commercially made automobiles. It had a four cylinder engine with seven horsepower and "one chug per telegraph pole"—all for $650! The advertising men pointed out, "This graceful and practical automobile will do the work of six horses at an average cost of $35 per year. Board alone for one horse costs $180 a year, so the economy is very evident."

People were being gradually brought around, and soon it became clear the automobile was here to stay. In 1902 the American Automobile Association was formed; the Rambler, a car later known as the Jeffrey, appeared on the national scene; Studebaker built its first electric car; Packard patented the H-slot gearshift; and the Ohio Automobile Company became the Packard Motor Car Company. Automobiles were turning from fancy to fact, but there were problems with these new "balky" machines.

For one thing, the roads were not made for autos as shown by

Main Street looking north in the late 1920s, when the street was wider and cars could park in the center.

the following item from the local paper: "Street Superintendent Enos has had a force of men at work this week hauling the mud off the street that is carried in from the country on the beet wagons."

Horses were scared to death of these lurching, belching, noisy contraptions. Wagons were upset and passengers spilled out of carriages as the animals rebelled. But horses gradually became accustomed, to some extent, and the roads were improved. James A. Linscott, referred to earlier, was running for re-election to the board of supervisors in the fall of 1902. He had held the position for eight years but had lost to Edward White in the previous election.

The people will not go back to the old order of dust and uneven roadways. Mr. Linscott is alive and up-to-date on all matters pertaining to road construction and he is able to stand for Pajaro's interest at all times in the Board of Supervisor's room.
—The *Pajaronian*, October 2, 1902

Linscott won the election as did George C. Pardee, the Republican from Alameda, as governor of California.

The Hare and the Tortoise.

Changing a flat tire.

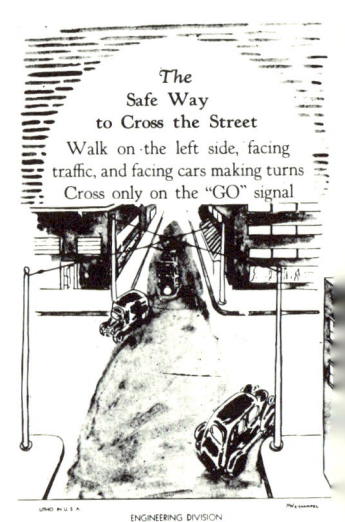

An imaginative photographer captured the stark contrast between a broken-down stagecoach, which he dated 1860, and a 1912 model of the horseless carriage.

Main Street looking south, c. 1930. Notice sign on left showing the price of gas to be twenty-one cents a gallon. At the extreme right is the Lyman Cox home.

APPLETON GARAGE

WATSONVILLE

Phones 163-164

Claim Check Nº 4660

 ROY WITTSCHEN

Signs at the Watsonville Garage (later Jones Garage, now the site of Rasco's) in 1913 gave the price of gas at twenty cents a gallon, cash or charge, and stated that all bills paid by the fifth of the month would receive a five percent discount.

In February of 1903, Dr. P. K. Watters, a local physician, purchased a handsome doctor's coupe which was ideal for stormy weather and night calls to his patients in the Pajaro Valley. According to his granddaughter, Helen Watters Bergman, this was the second car to be delivered in Watsonville. Charles Mackrell again made news when he purchased the *Examiner* and *Bulletin* routes and began delivery of newspapers in his Oldsmobile—the first time for newspapers to be delivered by auto in the Pajaro Valley. In San Francisco, more automobile news hit the headlines as H. Nelson Jackson left on May 23 for the first automobile trip across the United States. He drove a two-cylinder Winton and arrived in New York on July 26. In November of 1903, a Winton touring car arrived in Watsonville:

A. E. Joy of the wide-awake real estate firm of Joy & Maher, in this city, arrived here this morning with his recently purchased automobile and to express it mildly the machine is a thing of beauty. The automobile is one of the noted Winton 25-horsepower double cylinder touring cars and arrived from the Eastern factory only a few days ago. It has two speeds and two powerful emergency brakes. The upholstery is of rich color and high grade. The seating capacity is for six persons but five can ride with the greatest of comfort. Mr. Joy purchased the machine after having consulted with several leading business men of San Francisco, owners of other makes of high grade machines who advised a Winton. Also, he received the advice from Barney Oldfield by whom he was taken for a ride in a Winton. Mr. Oldfield uses one of these cars in his trials against the records, and his present world's record was made with a Winton. The car is complete in equipment with the exception of a powerful search-light, overlooked in the shipping, to arrive later.... (We have become dissatisfied with the newspaper business since observing that hustlers in the real estate business can ride in touring cars while we have to hoof it through the mud. Editor.)
—The *Pajaronian*, November 19, 1903

Speed limits in 1903 were eight miles an hour in town and fifteen miles out on the open road. The Buick Motor Company was founded this same year and the Model A Ford was introduced to the public. The two-seater sold for $800 and the four-seater for $900. Ford produced 1,700 cars during its first year of business.

Still, the country was not prepared for the automobile. There were no gas stations, no road maps, no motels, and gas had to be purchased at the local hardware or drug store. It was the rugged and daring who drove these machines over roads made for horse travel and trails rutted by the covered wagons. But all this was changing and the "buggy without a horse" was here to stay. The local paper noted in 1904 that on a given Sunday a Watsonville family drove to Santa Cruz in their automobile, attended church and returned home the same day, and a man drove from Watsonville to Monterey in his Rambler auto in three and a half hours!

W. H. White, local manager of the Earl Fruit Company, arrived last evening at 7:30 o'clock from San Francisco in an Oldsmobile which he will henceforth manipulate in chasing orchardists in the interest of the company he represents. The fifty miles from San Francisco to San Jose was covered in two hours and ten minutes, the chauffeur driving. The trip from the Garden City to Watsonville was not whirled off at the same rate of speed, however, as Mr. White insisted on handling the throttle himself after agreement with the chauffeur to hold her down to six miles an hour.

—The *Pajaronian*, 1905

In 1908 a local automobile club was formed with twenty-two charter members. Officers were: President, Dr. P. K. Watters; Vice-President, James Sheehy; Treasurer, W. D. Gulick; and Secretary, W. S. Foltz. By now the speed limit was up to twelve miles per hour in town and automobiles were becoming more common on the city's streets.

Mateo Lettunich returned from San Francisco last evening with his new Buick touring car. Nick Lettunich was at the wheel and the other occupants of the car were M. N. Lettunich of San Francisco and Frank Marisch of Goldfield, Nevada. M. N. Lettunich, whose large business interests in this valley call him to Watsonville frequently, has also joined the auto motorists ranks and has purchased a Buick "white streak."

—The *Pajaronian*, June 24, 1909

The car registration law went into effect in 1905 and during the first six months of 1909 there were more cars sold than the total for 1908. In Watsonville there were two automobile garages listed in the city directory—the Century Garage at 450 Main Street and

Cornell Tractor Company at West Lake and Walker in 1947. The cashier was Stella Zar.

the Watsonville Garage, 464-468 Main Street. As shown by the following article, all was not smooth sailing with the motorist:

Mayor Was In the Flying Machine—Yesterday Chief of Police Albright notified all of the local garages and autoists that the recent infractions of the speed law in Watsonville would not be tolerated any longer. This morning one of the first violators of the 12 mile an hour ordinance in the city of Watsonville was Guy L. Bailey of Berkeley, a mechanical engineer, visiting friends here, who was accompanied by Mayor J. A. Linscott.... He cheerfully paid the $6 fine imposed, but characterized the ordinance as ridiculous—wherein the people who have to walk do not agree with him.

—The *Pajaronian*, March 18, 1909

In 1910 gasoline was selling for eleven cents a gallon. By 1915 the Pajaro Valley had 337 automobiles, including fifty-three

Fords, thirty-seven Buicks, thirty-three Maxwells, and two Studebakers. New laws and regulations were imposed upon the motorist, and the following is an answer to these by an "irate" motorist who obviously felt these new restrictions were ridiculous:

Upon discovering or approaching a team, the automobilist must stop offside and cover his machine with a blanket to correspond with the scenery. On approaching a corner where he cannot see the road ahead, the automobilist must stop not less than 100 yards from the turn, toot his horn, ring a bell, fire a revolver, haloo and send up three rockets at intervals of five minutes. In case a horse will not pass an automobile, the automobilist will take the machine apart as rapidly as possible and conceal the parts in the grass . . .

Yes, the car with the "treacherous back-kick" was definitely past the novelty stage. These early-day autos are now some of the highest priced cars on the road, having been lovingly restored to their former elegance by their modern day owners.

The most recent addition to the local ranks of devoted autoists is Architect William H. Weeks. He has recently purchased a handsome Maxwell touring car. Will handles the balky machine in a finished style. He "caught on" rapidly and did not need much coaching.

Frank Oliver Buys a New Hupmobile—L. Fergoda reports the delivery of a new Hupmobile touring car to F. E. Oliver of this city. He took Mr. Oliver and family to San Francisco the fore part of the week and they drove back in their new car. Mr. Oliver is more than pleased with his purchase.
—*Evening Pajaronian*, August 25, 1922

The only way to solve the traffic problems of the country is to pass a law that only paid-for cars are allowed to use the highways. That would make traffic so scarce we could use our boulevards for children's playgrounds.
—Will Rogers

Main Street looking south in 1932. Pep Creamery is on the right.

Steinhauser and Eaton Drug Store on Main Street near Second, during the flood of 1911.

Chapter Nine

Businesses

In addition to manufacturing new hats, Mr. Ashton makes men's and women's old hats over into new ones and sends each woman away with an individual style of head gear which she is in no danger of meeting on another's head at the first corner she turns.
—*Evening Pajaronian*, 1931

Many profit-seeking enterprises sprang up in Watsonville down over the years. Some lasted a lot longer than others; some were hardly able to get off the ground. In 1898 and 1899, some of the businesses listed in the Watsonville City Directory were: Carl Rappe, jeweler, 317 Main Street; Alexander & Sons, 349-351 Main Street; Elite Chop House—"the only 15¢ meal in town"—188 Main Street; Burland Bros., Undertakers and Embalmers, 17 West Third Street; James Sheehy, dealer in groceries, fine wines and liquors, dairy produce, hay and wood, fruit and vegetables and agent for Cushing's celebrated squirrel poison, corner Main and First Streets; the El Dorado Meat Market, H. C. Peckham, proprietor, 427 Main Street; Emkay Candy Factory, maker of French candies, 19A East Third Street; Lewis & Son, surveyors, office over Bank of Watsonville; Romaldo Chaballa, manufacturer of the "best beef and chicken tamales on the coast," 232 Main Street; Eclipse Livery Stable, Thomas Kennedy, proprietor, 235 Main Street; and Joe's Saloon, Joseph Piroja, proprietor, best brands of wines, liquors and cigars on hand, fine billiard table and card rooms, Guioco delle Boccie, 265 Main Street.

——— • ———

At the corner of Ford and Main streets once stood the Mariposa Building and Saloon. In January of 1881 someone set fire to the then abandoned building which was owned by Charles Ford at the time. Frank Aldridge, who had just sold his flouring mill in Corralitos, purchased the property and built a three-story structure to house his Golden Sheaf Flouring Mill. When finished in July of 1881, the mill was turning out 130 barrels of flour a day and three teams of horses were kept busy hauling the flour to the depot. After arriving in San Francisco, many of the sacks of flour were shipped

Daly Brothers Store, September 27, 1911, at the corner of Main Street and Maple Avenue. Left to right: Minnie Storm, unknown, Nick Strazicich, Florence Joy, Frieda Steglich, Mamie Davidson.

to Liverpool, England. The mill flourished for a number of years, but it, like many others in California, was hit by disaster when the English companies refused to pay for the flour. After the mill closed down, local merchant Otto Stoesser purchased the property and used the buildings for storage.

Frank Aldridge, owner of the flour mill, was also an ordained minister in the Christian Church and served as pastor on Sundays. He was elected to the State Legislature in 1895, was married three times, and had a total of thirteen children. He died in 1900 at the age of seventy-four.

——— • ———

Among the fairer sex in business was Carrie Clausen who, in 1906, began her apprenticeship as a milliner under the guidance of Miss Nellie Butman, whose shop was located in the Odd Fellow's Building. In 1916 Miss Clausen became the owner of the store and

Rohrback store on San Juan Road. At far left is Judge Daniel Webster Rohrback. Second from right is Constable Gil Cano of Pajaro Township. Circa 1910.

Carrie M. Clausen, circa 1909.

Carrie Clausen.

was to design many a hat for local women, molding the material on hat forms, then tailoring, tucking and stitching the fitting. She specialized in hats to fit the customer's personality and, as the years went by and styles changed, she converted many of the hats to fit the new trends.

In 1926 Carrie moved her shop to 445 Main Street and continued in her business until 1940 at which time she retired—but not for long, as she was soon to be working again as head of the millinery department of Ford's Department Store. Her many friends showed their affection in 1954 when they banded together and presented the popular milliner with a trip to Hawaii. Miss Clausen died in 1964 at the age of seventy-five and she was mourned by many. Besides her business interests, she was active in the Soroptomist Club, Rebekah Lodge, the Pajaro Valley Historical Association, Native Daughters of the Golden West, and the Presbyterian Church.

——— • ———

A. Lewis & Co.'s Packing House—On Monday last we visited the above establishment, situated at Willoughby's place about four miles from town, and were surprised that so much had been accomplished since the business was commenced, on the 9th of August last. A pork packing house has long been needed in this valley for nearly all of the salt pork, bacon and hams used in this place and vicinity, have been imported, but very soon Messers. Lewis and Company will be enabled to fully supply the demand of this section. The company now kills about twenty hogs per day. The slaughter house, salting room, pickling room, lard room, packing room, smoke house and, in fact, all the appointments of the place are convenient and neatly kept. Their hogs are fattened on grain, and all are in fine condition for killing. We doubt not that with the experienced management the institution now has, that it will become an important and valuable manufactory, not only supplying the local market but all the neighboring towns.

—The *Pajaronian*, 1870

This business was sold when Mr. Lewis moved to Marysville and the building was torn down several years ago out on Riverside Road.

——— • ———

Daley and Quinn Bros. Meat Market, 203 Main Street, in 1905.

Steinhauser and Eaton Drug Store.

The town has been full of drummers the past week. The promise of good season makes them bold in their advances. Eleven cigar men in town at one time last week, they all met in a certain cigar store, and all commenced talking at once. The proprietor of that store is now afflicted with partial deafness, and a decided aversion to cigar runners.

—The *Pajaronian*, April 25, 1878

———   •   ———

When the Porter building was constructed in 1903, Daly Brothers opened its doors to the public in October of that year; the store was located in the corner portion of the new building at Main and Maple. This marked the beginning of Daly's in Watsonville which was founded by Denis Joseph Daly and his brother, Pat Daly, who had been born in Ireland where their father operated a dry goods store. While still young men, the Daly boys migrated to the United States, first settling in San Francisco and then coming on to Watsonville.

In 1914 Daly Brothers moved their store up the street into the newly built Lettunich Building, again being located on the ground floor. The business stayed at this location until 1929, when they moved to 345 Main Street, now the site of Diehm's. Denis Daly purchased the Newman house on Maple Avenue which is now owned by Mr. and Mrs. Frank Peters, who have recently painted the outside.

Pat Daly died in 1930, and Denis died in 1953 at the age of eighty-six. He had been quite an athlete in the early 1900s and was once the Pacific Coast handball champion. He was also known for his dry wit and good humor. After his death, Denis Daly, Jr. was in charge of the store, having joined the firm in 1940. Daly Brothers closed its doors to the public in 1969, having been a vital part of the community for sixty-three years.

———   •   ———

The dry goods, clothing and shoe stores of this city have entered into an agreement whereby they will open at 7:30 o'clock every morning and will close promptly at 9 o'clock on every Saturday evening, this to be in vogue until June 1. Heretofore these stores opened at 7 o'clock every morning but these merchants have seen the folly of the extra half hour and decided on the above agreement . . .

—*Evening Pajaronian*, February 11, 1916

ITS TIME TO GO TO

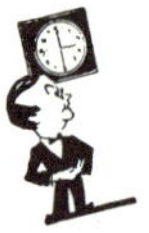

THE WHITE HOUSE
For Your
BEER, WINE & LUNCH

229 MAIN STREET
WATSONVILLE, CALIF.

PHONE 864
C. LOGAN

P. M. Andrews,

CONTRACTOR AND BUILDER

Jobbing a Specialty.

Estimates Given on Short Notice.

SHOP, 444 MAIN STREET.   TELEPHONE, 205.
RESIDENCE, 32 SUDDEN STREET.

ECLIPSE 1899
Livery Stable,

Watsonville, California.

Wm. H. KENNEDY, — — Proprietor.

Horses Boarded by Day, Week or Month.
Hack at all hours.   Terms Reasonable.

235 Main Street   Phone, Main 241.

June 3, 1920

Professional Cards

DENTIST

DR. S. JEWETT
DENTIST

Phone 418W   Cooper Bldg.

PHYSICIANS

Office Phone 560
DR. OTTO H. GOTSCH
Ostheopathic Physician
Laboratory Diagnosis a Specialty
Rooms 6-8-10   Stoesser Block

VETERINARY SURGEON

DR. W. J. C. RAMSEY
• Veterinary Surgeon
Office: E. Lake Ave., near Main
Phone: Office 108; House 442R

ATTORNEYS AT LAW

WYCKOFF & GARDNER
Attorneys-at-Law
Room 423, 4th Floor Lettunich
Block, Phone 81

D. F. MAHER,
Attorney
Room 414   Lettunich Building
Phone 200
Notary in Office.

JAMES A. HALL,
Attorney-at-Law
Room 418 Fourth Floor
Lettunich Building

ADAM BARBER
Attorney-at-Law
Room 419, Fourth Floor
Bank of Watsonville Building

CLAY W. SEEVERS
Attorney-at-Law
Pajaro Valley Bank Building
Phone 328   Notary Public

1901

Nov. 21

Mr Chas Rowe
To **WYCKOFF & ASTON, DR.**
Funeral Directors and Embalmers

Tel. Black 31

I. O. O. F. Block

19 East Third St.

$45.00
10.00
6.50
2.50
$64.00

ANNOUNCEMENT
SPRING AND SUMMER 1916

A BRILLIANT SHOWING OF THE VERY LATEST FASHIONS AND FABRICS FOR THE NEW SEASON HAVE NOW ARRIVED. BEAUTIFUL NOVELTIES, BANJO STRIPES AND ELEGANT STAPLES AFFORD YOU A PLEASING CHOICE OF SUITINGS, OVERCOATINGS, VESTINGS AND TROUSERINGS. EVERY STYLE IS GUARANTEED ALL PURE WOOL.
YOU WILL RECEIVE AS USUAL, PERSONAL AND CAREFUL ATTENTION AND YOUR CUSTOM TAILORING REQUIREMENTS WILL BE INTERPRETED IN AN EXPERT AND PROMPT MANNER.

VERY TRULY YOURS

VINCENT A. FETZMAN
THE TAILOR
LETTUNICH BLDG. 2ND FLOOR,
WATSONVILLE, CAL.

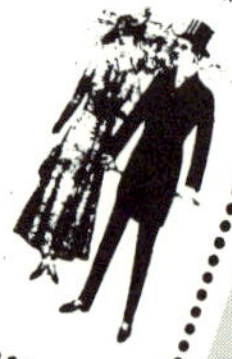

Steinhauser & Eaton Drug, located at 325 Main Street and now owned by Harry Johnson, was founded in 1874 as the Watsonville Drug Store, then located at 313 Main Street. Elliott Steinhauser and Roy Eaton purchased the store in 1899, thus the change of name. Mr. Eaton was a graduate of Watsonville High School and Northwestern University, where he graduated with high honors as a chemist. Elliott Steinhauser came to Watsonville from Oakland, California, where he had been a pharmacist for some years. He was married to Jean Weeks, sister of architect William Weeks.

In 1908 Mr. Steinhauser was riding his bike down Main Street when he was kicked by a horse and knocked down. His left arm was broken, which resulted in a long and expensive period of medical treatment, but his arm could not be restored to its former usefulness. Selling his interest in the drug store to his partner, he then embarked on a very successful career in the real estate business. Mr. Steinhauser died in 1925. Roy Eaton died in 1968.

Other owners have been Ray Palmtag, William Burgoin, Owen T. Knowlton, and Archie Hall prior to Mr. Johnson's purchase in 1963. One hundred and six years after the founding of this drug store, it is still a vital part of the local business community.

——— • ———

Harold and Lou Foote opened their first creamery in Watsonville in the year of 1924. It was known as the Independent Creamery and was at 8-14 East Lake Avenue. In 1930 a new plant was erected on Main Street and the firm was incorporated as the Pep Creamery, with other stores being located in Monterey, Hollister, Santa Cruz and Salinas.

On August 27, 1939, a new Pep Creamery building opened to the public in Watsonville on the corner of East Beach and Carr streets. The $10,000 structure boasted of glass bricks on two corners of the building, "which were rounded to carry out the modernistic theme." Open from 10:00 A.M. until the early hours of the morning, the creamery featured a serve-yourself idea—the customer could place his order with an employee and pick up his own tray—or there was service to your car.

Inside the creamery were U-shaped counters plus tables and up to ninety people could be seated at one time. Another feature of the new eatery were two table tops on which patrons (mostly

California Restaurant at 259 Main Street. Andrew Strazicich is behind the bar and Johnny Corr is seated at back table. The restaurant was located in the Dondero block built in 1893, across from the present City Hall.

high school students) could carve to their heart's delight. These carved table tops were then hung on the wall and credited to the class of 1940. But by 1944 the building was sold and became the home of McDowell Printing Service. In 1947 it was sold to Ed Kimmel and Doug Evans and the name was changed to Service Printers and is still that today, now owned by John Leeson. Pep Creamery was then located at 433 Main Street.

——— • ———

Some businesses had trouble which was a little different from that of other establishments.

There was a series of fights in the Old Corner Saloon, Tuesday evening, that had neither referee, bottle holder, nor a police officer as sideshows. The fights were outside of ring rules, and the battle ground was from the interior of the saloon to the edge of the sidewalk. At one time a trio combination scrap was in progress, and clothes and arms were flying in bewildering muddle. The combatants were past masters in the use of dialect profanity. It was a disgraceful scene. Prolonged blasts on the police whistle did not call forth a star decorated guardian of the peace. They were not there. Not even allurements of the circus and the calliope band should allure the blue-coated guardians of the peace, during the hours of their beat from the lamp lighted avenues of the commercial part of our city. Tuesday night's scrap was a disgrace to any community and it should not be duplicated.

—The *Pajaronian*, September 27, 1894

OPENINGS AND NEW OWNERS

1883—"Frank Kitchen has opened an ice cream saloon in the tent recently put up next door to Cooper's store. He favored this office with a sample of his ice cream last week. It was delicious." —The *Pajaronian*

1879—"Messrs. Merchant and Hagerty have opened a soap factory on Main Street, below McLeans' blacksmith shop, and are now prepared to fill all orders. Their soap is good for all purposes claimed."—The *Pajaronian*

1910—"The new real estate firm under title of the Farm and Forest Realty Company, with E. Steinhauser as manager, has opened for business at 320 Main Street in the rooms occupied for a while as headquarters for the Apple Annual association..." —The *Evening Pajaronian*

1969—"The Office Supply Co., 440 Main St., will have new owners July 1. After 20 years of ownership, Jack and Stella Haskin are selling the store to Theodore (Ted) Taylor and his wife, Mary..."—The *Register-Pajaronian*

This Card Good for 5c in Trade
— at —
YOUNG'S COFFEE STORE
— Located in —
SMITH'S METROPOLITAN CASH MARKET, Third Street, Watsonville

We are taking this method of giving you the benefit of advertising our High Grade Coffee. This card properly signed with name and address entitles the holder to one pound of YOUNG'S KONA BLEND 40c Coffee for 35c, or one pound of YOUNG'S 3-4-1 SPECIAL 35c Coffee for 30c.

WE HELP YOU—YOU HELP US

Void After

Name

Address

1929 advertisement—"Reopening The Owl recreation parlor - Sat., Oct. 26th - under the old reliable management formerly known as the Pajaro Valley Pool Room, 237 Main St. Training quarters for the Watsonville Athletic Club ... Come in and see the new Billiard Room and watch the local boys train."—The *Pajaronian*

1964—"Watsonville's newest shopping center, East Lake Village, will be open Wednesday. ... The project, six months in the building, is the enterprise of Eddie Phillips and Luke Vidak, who began working together in Watsonville 26 years ago as grocery store employees and since have become shopping center owners and developers ... ."—The *Pajaronian*

——— • ———

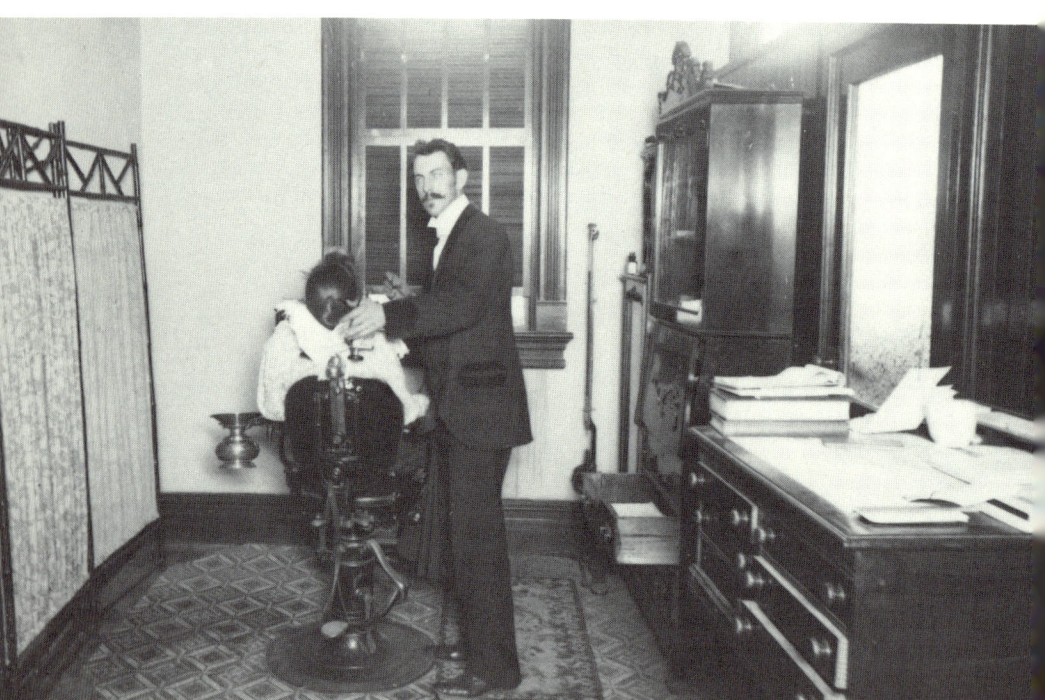

Dr. Charles Butterfield in his dental office in the Peck Block.

Dr. Butterfield and his musical family. This picture was taken at Peck and Union streets, with the IOOF Hall and the Opera House in the background.

DR. CHARLES BUTTERFIELD

By use of nitrous oxide gas Dr. Butterfield is prepared to extract teeth. Absolutely painless and without danger.

—The *Pajaronian*, 1889

Charles Butterfield was a well-known figure in Watsonville—he was what one might call a "traveling" dentist. Whenever he was going to be in town there would be an ad in the local paper announcing the dates and times he would be available. The whole Butterfield family were very talented in the musical field. In 1907 they gave a concert at the Odd Fellow's Hall and the orchestra consisted of Dr. Butterfield, trombone; Beatrice, his wife, first violin; Bernice, piano; Marian, cornet; and Dorothy, violin. "They are but five—small and tall—in the Butterfield family of concert entertainers, but they are equal to holding an audience down in fine shape with artistic selections."

Dr. Butterfield was born on a ranch in the Chittenden area, the son of Mr. and Mrs. Joseph Butterfield. Mrs. H. F. Blohm, of Aromas, was his sister. When he was in Watsonville, his office was in the Peck Block at Main and Peck streets and his home was at 236 Lake Avenue, where neighbors could hear the family practicing on many an evening.

On a visit to Watsonville in 1928, after the doctor's retirement to Calaveras County, he told of the disbanding of the family orchestra as the members had married and scattered to all parts of the state. Charles Butterfield died in 1934 but many can still remember him dressed as Uncle Sam and marching in the Fourth of July parades with his family, all playing instruments. It was quite a talented family.

Dr. Butterfield is the composer of a song, "Love's Wireless," composed by Dr. C. L. Butterfield of this city and his son-in-law, S. J. Mustol of San Jose; Dr. Butterfield writing the words and Mr. Mustol composing the music. The song was recently sung at a gathering at Santa Clara University by a prominent San Francisco vocalist and made a big hit...."

—*Evening Pajaronian*, May 4, 1915

Chapter Ten

Bicycling Craze

The Pajaro Wheel Club has rented the old "schoolroom" in the Opera House block, and has fitted it up for a club room. The furnishings are in good taste and the handsome new billiard tables are an attraction that will appeal to every member of the organization. The club has taken a field that has long been open in Watsonville and the young men propose to have and maintain an organization that will be a credit to themselves and the town.
—The *Pajaronian*, February 2, 1893

The first president of the Wheelman's Club was A. W. Cox; George Jessen was secretary and Charles Palmtag treasurer. "Wheeling is on the increase and the club has come to stay," the *Pajaronian* reported. Their first party, held in May of that year, was hailed as a "gratifying success" as the some twenty members and their guests enjoyed refreshments and talk of the bicycling world.

Bicycling became THE sport that year as riders came out in force on a balmy Sunday, wheeling their way over rutted dirt roads on the rubber-tired vehicles.

C. A. Palmtag and George Tuttle with their wheels.

This post card was mailed in November of 1904. The legend at the bottom of the picture says, "Look before you leap."

The bicycle fever has taken Watsonville worse than an epidemic of the mumps. One of the latest debutants on the "winged wheel" is A. Newman. He showed great speed.

—The *Pajaronian*, April 6, 1893

The ladies were also out cycling, and "bloomers" soon became "all the rage" in 1894, and Watsonville was hailed as the "banner town" on the coast for lady bicyclists. But all was not easy sailing; complaints such as the following appeared in the local newspaper:

Is Watsonville's bicycle sidewalk ordinance for use or for ornament? If for the former purpose let it be enforced without "fear" or "favor." If for ornament we would suggest that it be properly engrossed (*sic*) and framed and be considered a start for a city art gallery.

—The *Pajaronian*

Christy Redman had a bicycle novelty in the shape of a sail which was attached to the steering post of his bike. He made record-breaking time out Beach Road when the wind was with him. Chief Engineer Wilson had a fire alarm system connected to his bicycle so that when the fire alarm sounded, his bicycle bell would strike the number of the box and set the wheels in motion. "The Chief is going to be to the front even if he has to put wings on his bike."

In March of 1895, the cycling brigade of the Wheelman's Club mounted their wheels "one dreary morn" and pedaled over to Santa Cruz in less than three hours. Vic Tuttle captured the county record for a mile at 2:57—on a poor track. While at the county seat, the cyclists viewed the double-headed woman being exhibited on the courthouse lot—a sideshow relic of the Midwinter Fair held in San Francisco the year before.

Bicycles were selling like "hot cakes"; ministers were even encouraging people to ride, saying it was "good for their souls."

George P. Martin, the live bicycle agent, who sold 22 wheels this season, has ordered five more Sterlings shipped direct from Chicago. These wheels, built like watches, are popular all the time. Martin's ability as a salesman has been recognized by the Sterling Company who have appointed him coast agent for their wheel. He also carries the Phoenix, Rambler and Crawford bicycles.

—The *Pajaronian*, April 18, 1895

Martin's store was located at 320 Main Street in the former Peck Block. His main business was that of a jeweler and he also carried a line of stationery. J. A. Baxter was another local bicycle agent whose ad read: "Don't ride a Cleveland Bicycle unless you are prepared to catch the 'Cleveland Fever.' It is awfully contagious—but it is healthy. Did you ever see a Cleveland rider who wasn't robust and happy?"

One cyclist did not fare too well, though:

A cyclist and the earthquake shock met, near the orphanage, last Sunday noon. Both passed on, but the shock went the greater distance. The biker went through the air about fifteen feet.

—The *Pajaronian*, June 24, 1897

In 1898, you could purchase a "keen" pair of bicycle shoes for a dollar and a half at Pena and Hall's which was located in the Cooper Block at Main and West Beach, now the site of Monterey Savings and Loan. And how about the cost of your wheel? Columbia chainless sold for seventy-five dollars or, without chain, sixty dollars. The Hartford went for thirty-five dollars and the Vedette was a bargain at twenty-five. In February of 1900,

"The Good Boys of Ford's Store." Left to right, Al Cupid, George P. (Ginks) Martin, and Louie McClean. Seated, Arnie Cox. This picture was taken in the nineties.

J. A. Baxter advertised in the *Pajaronian*: "It is so very rare indeed that any one firm has the opportunity to represent so many manufacturers of Standard Bicycles as we do for the season of 1900. The Cleveland, the Crescent, the Stearn, the Sterling and the Mars—with only part of the above agencies we sold nearly one hundred bicycles in 1899. Prices range from $22.50 to $50.00. Imagine, you readers that paid $150.00 for a 'bone shaker' seven or eight years ago, of getting a wheel ONE HUNDRED TIMES BETTER for only $22.50." It is interesting to note that now, the Valley Sport Shop on East Lake Avenue averages 300 sales a year on bicycles.

Baxter's store was located at 401 Main Street, before the Charles Ford Company's store was extended to the corner. He also stocked hardware, spring wagons, coal, ammunition, oil, glass, wallpaper, paint, and farm implements! Yes, the bicycle was here to stay—at least until the "horseless carriage" made its debut on the scene. The change from the high bicycle to the lower frame model made for safer cycling and an easier bike to handle.

Pierce Cyclery at 464 Main Street in 1908. J. A. Seitz was the proprietor.

Bicycle races became very popular, such as the one in Salinas in April of 1895, a ten-mile race in which three men from Watsonville entered—E. Mahlgren, Victor Tuttle and Ed Mauk. Mahlgren won the first prize, a gold stop watch and a medal, and Tuttle came in second, winning a silver stop watch.

The "wheel" was a means of transportation for some. Local architect William Weeks would take one on the train with him when working on a job out of town and use it as a means of conveyance. Sometimes it was easier for the local doctor to dash off on his bicycle than to take the time to hitch the horses to the wagon or buggy. But you had to watch out for the bicycle thief: "Some individual with an abnormally developed case of 'nerve' stole C. S. Bachelder's new chainless Stearns bicycle Saturday night from in front of A. L. Bixby's grocery store," and "Last Tuesday afternoon between the hours of 2 and 4 o'clock someone took a bicycle belonging to I. H. Tuttle's daughter, Ione, from the Primary school building and Mr. Tuttle spent about two hours before he located the wheel. Bicycle stealing seems to be a popular past-time in this city lately and a term in jail for some of

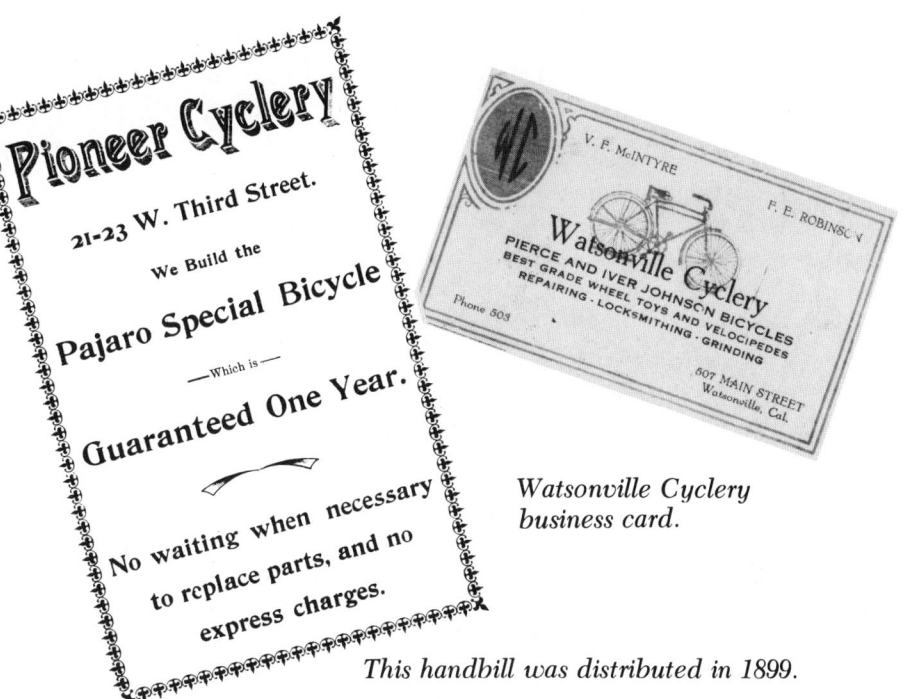

Watsonville Cyclery business card.

This handbill was distributed in 1899.

the guilty ones would doubtless have a tendency to remedy the existing evil. One hardly dares to let his bike out of his sight these days."

Larger quarters were needed for the Pajaro Valley Wheelman's Club so they moved to the Peck Block and held their meetings in rooms upstairs—a big "blowout" was given in the new quarters. Bicycle racks appeared on the streets and down at the high school, "large enough to accommodate up to 50 wheels." Newspaper carriers used the "winged wheel" for delivering the local news, but they and other cyclists were constantly being chased off the sidewalks:

Dr. Charles Beebe was the first to contribute $5.00 to the city under Marshal Trafton's administration, for the privilege of riding a bicycle on the sidewalks. The doctor took the matter good-naturedly and congratulated the Marshal upon his determination to enforce the city ordinances. Justice to all and special privileges to none is Marshal Trafton's motto.

—The *Pajaronian*, November 16, 1900

With the advent of the motorcycle and the automobile, the bicycle hit a decline. Americans had new toys to play with and the bicycle was relegated to the background.

The rise of the automobile and decline of the bicycle are shown in a census bulletin just issued at Washington. In 1905 the number of factories producing bicycles was 101 against 312 in 1900... Many of the establishments which once made nothing but bicycles had engaged in the making of automobiles.
—*Evening Pajaronian*, May 13, 1907

Bicycling did take a back seat to the newer modes of transportation but was still a popular vehicle.

There is some ambition on the part of Freedom to produce a trio of relay bicycle riders that can knock the pedals off from any trio to be jumped up in the Watsonville sagebrush. To that end the Freedoms have challenged a pick-up team composed of ex-members of the Holligans and Tribunes. The line-up will be, that is if they line up—Tribunes - Louis Trabing, Archie Blohm and William Downing. Freedom - William Lasher, Gus Nistetter and Walter Gleason.
—*Evening Pajaronian*, July 30, 1908

When city ordinance number 468 went into effect on July 24, 1939, Charles Hushbeck was first in line for bicycle license number one. The ordinance stated that all owners of bicycles were to pay an annual fee of fifty cents to the police department in return for a license plate to be attached to the owner's bicycle. Chief of Police Matt Graves stated that violation of the ordinance would bring a maximum fine of $299 and maximum jail term of ninety days.

———— • ————

H. C. Peckham has about completed arrangements for the building of a quarter-mile bicycle track at Peterson's Point, on College Lake. Henry is doing everything possible to make his College Lake venture a success and in building a bicycle track at Peterson's Point he is deserving of the praise and support of the many bikers in this valley.
—The *Pajaronian*, August 1, 1895

Chapter Eleven

James Waters and the Pajaro Valley Nursery

James Waters has lately leased for a term of years, with the privilege of buying, that fine piece of land known as the Sudden tract. Mr. Waters will, this Winter, move his trees, shrubbery, etc., and in fact all that composes his present extensive nursery business, to the larger tract mentioned, where he proposes to enter into the nursery business more extensively than ever. He will also engage extensively in floriculture, having already made arrangements for a large and beautiful variety of exotics as well as new and rare shrubbery and trees. His stock of fruit trees is very extensive and choice, and his long experience, and excellent judgment and taste, is sufficient guarantee that the new nursery will be one of the most extensive as well as the finest on the coast.
—The *Pajaronian*, October 11, 1877

Somerset County, Maryland was the birthplace of James Waters on October 18, 1828. He and his father, his mother and younger sister having died, moved to Baltimore where young James attended school. At the age of sixteen he went into the carpentry business with his father and gained a thorough

James Waters.   *Malinda Short Waters.*

Back view of the home of Mr. and Mrs. James Waters in the late 1800s. Pictures courtesy Mrs. Philip Gilman, Jr.

The same view in 1930. Courtesy Mrs. Philip Gilman, Jr.

knowledge of the craft under his father's guiding hand. James set out for California in June of 1849 thinking to make his fortune in the gold fields. Arriving in San Francisco, he was offered a job as a carpenter for one dollar an hour and worked for about a year before going on to the mines, where he stayed for two years. Returning to San Francisco, he took up his carpentry trade, but the failure of the banking house of Page, Bacon and Company wiped out most of his savings. The year was 1855 and this is when Waters decided on moving to Santa Cruz, where he went into partnership with Thomas Beck, who was to become his brother-in-law. The men married sisters.

These two men were to fulfill a number of building contracts at the county seat, including the rebuilding of the Catholic Church after the 1857 earthquake and the construction of the county courthouse in 1866.

James Waters moved to the Pajaro Valley in 1859 and continued in the construction business with such local buildings as the Blackburn home, Stoesser Block, Fire Engine House, Hildreth Block, the first St. Patrick's Church, the Patrick Kelly home, and the James Rodgers home. Horticulture had long been an interest of Mr. Waters and when he purchased property located along the Salsipuedes Creek, he planted the first commercial apple orchard.

In 1860 James married Malinda Short in a small ranch house near Pinto Lake in the Amesti district. He and his bride moved into a house located on the property along the Salsipuedes Creek. The flood of 1862 completely wiped out his orchard and home. He sold the land to the Catholic Church and purchased property on East Fourth (Lake) Avenue.

This home built for James Rodgers in 1869 was designed by James Waters. The picture was taken in 1879 by E. J. Muybridge, "the famous view photographer and discoverer of the process by which instantaneous photographs were taken of running and trotting horses." Courtesy Mrs. Esther Rodgers.

With J. A. Blackburn as a partner in 1867 he planted five acres of nursery stock, and in 1873 he bought his partner's interest, becoming the sole proprietor. Upon purchasing twenty-seven acres from Captain Sudden he moved the nursery to what was then known as Sudden and Fourth streets, Watsonville. His next purchase consisted of fifty acres adjacent to the Sudden tract and the new property he set out in strawberries, but eight years later he planted the fifty acres to apples, from which large

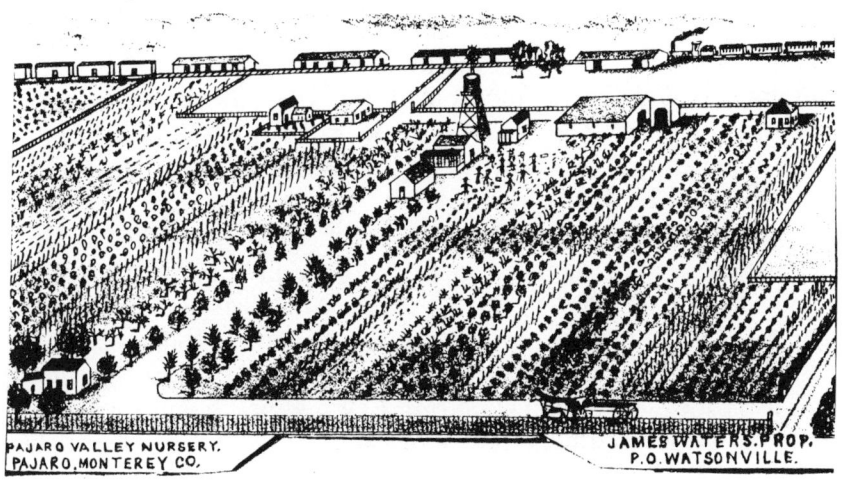

A 1900 lithograph.

crops have since been harvested. Meanwhile the nursery business had outgrown its quarters and he thereupon moved his plant to his new acquisition of fifty-two acres near the Pajaro depot in Monterey County. Later he purchased adjacent land, so that eighty acres were devoted to nursery stock.
—*History of Santa Cruz County* by Edward Martin, 1910

While living in a temporary home behind the Beck residence, Waters designed and built a new home at 336 East Lake Avenue on one and one-half acres purchased for $450. The property ran from East Lake back to East Third (Beach) and was considered, at that time, to be located on the "edge of town." On June 8, 1871 an article appeared in the *Pajaronian* describing the house:

The outside is finished in a highly ornamental and elaborate style, harmonious in all its details, and presents a most pleasant and home-like appearance ... The painting and graining is an excellent piece of work, artistic skill of no mean order being displayed in the graining, especially in the hall and stairway. To Messrs. Peckham & Judd belong the credit of this fine work ...

James Waters also found time to be active in the local community. He was one of the founders of the Bank of Watsonville in 1874, president of the Pajaro Valley Fair Association, a county supervisor for two years, and an active member of the Masons, the Knights' Templar, and the Society of California Pioneers. Mr. and Mrs. Waters had three children—Willie, who died at the age of twelve; Lola (Mrs. James Walker), who died at the age of twenty-five; and Adele (Della) Jackson, who later changed her name back to Waters. She had two children, William Waters and Hazel (Mrs. F. R. Ruppert).

Mr. Waters shipped the first strawberries from the valley to San Francisco and he named a variety, Linda, in honor of his wife.

At his nursery, every variety of seed and stone fruits were grown, along with the finest varieties of trees for shade or ornamental purposes. Many of the rare varieties were imported from France or other foreign countries. Finding that the nursery took up most of his time, Waters phased out of the construction

Will Waters, grandson of James Waters.

business, his last job being the Monterey County Court House in Salinas in 1878.

In 1893 the Waters Subdivision was opened on the old nursery grounds bounded by East Lake, Sudden, Palm and Madison:

> The Waters subdivision is in the full swing of a building boom, and is the liveliest part of the town. It is a most favorable residence location, and home seekers can find no better part of town in which to purchase a building lot. There are several lots of this tract unsold. For terms, etc., apply to James Waters.
>
> —The *Pajaronian*, April 11, 1895

Waters built a house at 335 Beach Street in 1894 which was occupied by his granddaughter, Hazel Ruppert. The small house was to be enlarged in the 1930s and is now owned by Mr. and Mrs. Ralph Stanton. The house on East Lake was added on to by architect Weeks in 1897 at a cost of $1,000. Other owners of the Waters house have been Warren Tuttle, Harry Parker, and the present owners, Dr. and Mrs. Philip Gilman, Jr.

James and Malinda Waters celebrated their fiftieth wedding anniversary on September 9, 1910 with a reception at their home from 2:00 to 5:00 P.M. Mr. Waters died just a little over a year later at the age of eighty-three; Malinda died in 1926.

> James Waters has purchased the Shetland pony and cart which was brought here some time since by a traveling photographer, and H. S. Fletcher has purchased a burro and cart in Santa Cruz. The Juveniles of the Waters and Fletcher families have been having high sport with their midget racers.
>
> —The *Pajaronian*, December 6, 1894

A group of local men at the Kelly-Thompson ranch. James Broadis is in the center of the picture.

One of Jim Broadis' hunting companions, Henry S. Fletcher, president of the Watsonville Bank, c. 1905.

Chapter Twelve

Jim Broadis—Runaway Slave

Across the pages of Watsonville's history have marched many rugged pioneers who came from all walks of life and from many parts of the world. One such man was James Broadis, sometimes spelled Brodis or Brodus. He was born a slave in Kentucky in 1833. According to his story as told to a local man, Lin Cleveland, his first master was more often drunk than sober and would have many a whipping administered to his slaves on the flimsiest of excuses.

One day the drunken master staggered into the room where the slaves were making lard, slipped on the greasy floor and fell into a hot drum of boiling lard. Whether he fell in or was tossed in one can only speculate, but anyway he was gone. Jim soon had a new master by the name of Broadis from Missouri, and that was when Jim acquired his last name.

When the cry of gold roared across the country, Jim and Mr. Broadis started the trek westward, joining up with a caravan of covered wagons. During the trip, which turned out to be a peaceful one, Jim spent much of his time hunting and fishing, thus supplying the travelers with fresh meat and fish. The two men landed in Marysville in the fall of 1849 and Mr. Broadis turned his hand to professional gambling and the beautiful gold nuggets, more often than not, came across the table his way. Jim served as cook and guard, watching over the growing pile of sacks of gold. After garnering quite a fortune, Mr. Broadis decided to return to his home in Missouri but didn't want to take Jim with him, so sold him over the gaming table for $1,600 in gold coin to a man by the name of Gunn.

Jim and his third owner went to the north fork of the Yuba River to a mining camp where he again served as cook and hunter. Someone in the camp finally told him that he was in a free state, and since Jim was always afraid of being taken back down south, he ran away. Men were sent out to find him, but Jim managed to elude them and eventually joined up with a band of Indians and traveled south, ending up in San Juan. He arrived in the Pajaro Valley in 1850 or 1851 and worked for a while on a ranch belonging to J. Bryant Hill.

Jim then became a teamster and hauled lumber from up in the mountains down to the planing mill in back of Ford's store. He also started a delivery service to people along his route, bringing them groceries and supplies for a small fee. According to the Santa Cruz County census, 1870, he was married to Maria (her first name was Ellen). The court records show that it was an "intermarriage"; she was born in Nova Scotia. Their children were listed as James, Jr., Tel, Priscilla, Ellen, Amanda, Harriet, and Mabel. The first three were the only ones who lived to maturity.

By a lot of hard work and saving as much as he could, Broadis was able to purchase twenty-six and one-half acres of land from Charles Ford and Lucius Sanborn in 1870 for $1,200. This property was located up on the heights at the northern end of Main Street in the High Street area. The hill was dubbed "Broadis Hill" or "Nigger Hill." There is a Broadis Street today located off Freedom Boulevard between Laurel and Prospect streets.

Over the years Broadis added to his land holdings and leased some of it out to other parties such as George Brewington, Jerome Milks, the Quinn brothers, and the Burland brothers. Jim's corn pasture was located where the Callaghan playground is now.

Broadis spent much of his spare time hunting and fishing with local men who valued his friendship and his expertise with the gun. Such men as the following were his sporting companions: H. S. Fletcher, Jim Williams, Ernest Cooper, Pete, John and Modesto Arano, Arthur and Tom Devine, John Williamson, Andy Beck, James Enemark, Al Cupid, Frank Briggs, Jim Struve, and Pete Rodriguez. One of Jim's closest friends was another Negro by the name of Dan Rodgers. The two men made a grisly find one day. Not having a well of his own, Jim would go across the road and use his neighbor's. One day Jim and Dan went to the well and found the body of William Roache, whose mysterious death was connected with the Sanchez treasure. (Note: see *Watsonville Yesterday.*)

Jim's home life became very turbulent and his wife sued for divorce, but it was denied in 1898. She was finally granted a divorce in March of 1906, the property having been divided the year before. Broadis could neither read nor write, and many of the legal documents bear his "mark" upon them. His wife moved to San Francisco, his two sons to San Jose, and his daughter up north Jim moved down to 173 Main Street into a small house.

Brodis' Home Sold To-Day—Purchased by syndicate of local capitalists. To be put on Market. Three hundred building lots to be added to list of desirable property. At 4 o'clock this afternoon the details of the purchase of the Brodis property were completed and it is now settled that this excellent residence site will be subdivided and placed on the market... The officers and stockholders (Watsonville Realty Company) are: Dr. Nat Green, president; Stephen Scurich, V.P.; Otto Raphael, Secretary; C. F. Langley, Wm. A. Trafton, Jas. Watt, H. A. Peckham, A. Faustino, C. Rappe and L. P. Cox. The new tract has been named the Watsonville Heights tract.
—*Evening Pajaronian*, March 3, 1905

When Jim Broadis died on June 28, 1906, many people thought that he had died a pauper; that he had buried his money in jars and it had been stolen. But not so, as he willed to his two sons, James and Tell, his estate which consisted of nearly twenty thousand dollars which had been kept in various banks in Watsonville and other towns. His daughter contested the will and it was finally settled in 1908 with Priscilla being awarded a portion of her father's estate.

James Broadis was indeed a pioneer of the Pajaro Valley, and, as the old saying goes, "he made good." But more than that, he was held in high regard and respected by many of the leading men of the town, who admired his determination and his ability. Next time you drive by Broadis Street, it may remind you of this runaway slave who helped settle the town of Watsonville.

Veterans Memorial Building, Watsonville, built in 1934.

Main Street looking south, c. 1950.

Chapter Thirteen

Shady Ladies and Sin City

The Shady Ladies were run out of town so many times it became ludicrous—each time it was for "the last time." An example is the ordinance, number twenty-one, passed by the city fathers in 1871 "to prohibit and suppress houses of prostitution, ill fame, disorderly houses and brothels within the town of Watsonville. It shall be unlawful to open or maintain any house of prostitution, ill fame, disorderly house or brothel within the corporate limits of the town of Watsonville..."

The following are from the *Pajaronian*:

Mary Peralto, who has been conducting an assignation house on Rodriguez Street, was arrested on Monday by Marshal Downing and Constable Hosgland and brought before Judge Swank. She was found guilty and sentenced to 25 days in the county jail.—1890

Two Japanese, a man and woman, who have been running a disreputable house on lower Main Street, were arrested Monday night by Marshal Downing. They were brought before Judge Swank on Tuesday morning and he found them guilty and fined them $25 apiece.—1890

Jean Daras, the keeper of a house of ill fame, was arrested last Saturday and charged with conducting a house of ill fame... Judge Swank sentenced Daras to six months in the county jail - the extreme penalty.—1892

The following appeared in the *Pajaronian* in 1906:

For the first time in the history of Watsonville, so far as known, this city is free from the public houses of prostitution. Their doors are closed; the inmates have sought more congenial surroundings. Thanks to the vigilance of our police officers every prostitute in town, with the exception of one who begged to be allowed to remain until this morning, in order to finish packing her belongings, left yesterday...

But a year later, in 1907, the ordinance forbidding houses of ill fame in the city was repealed, to the surprise of many who attended the meeting of the Board of Aldermen on a June evening, the thirteenth. "The opponents to the repeal of a certain measure who were expected to be on hand in a militant mood were conspicuous by their absence, and the course of municipal legislation flowed as smoothly onward as the water in Ex-Alderman Ostrander's pond (Lake Watsonville)."

This morning Mr. Polito and Mr. Valliant, two men who were caught in a raid on a house in the underworld on the 14th inst., pleaded guilty in Justice Wallace's court. The judge put on a stern manner and with dignity informed them that as this was their first offense he would be lenient with them and would make it only $20 each.
—*Register Pajaronian*, November 20, 1907

The red-light houses were also known as "play pens," "houses of ill repute," "bawdy houses," "brothels," etc. Locally, these houses were generally in the Union Street area, and, as of this writing, one is still standing on the corner of Union and Riverside but has been shut down by the city. It had been used for years as a rooming house. In November of 1914, the following appeared in the local paper:

Local Redlight District Closing—As a result of the passage of the Redlight Abatement Act the local red-light district, tenderloin section, *hoi polloi*, or whatever one chooses to call it, is starting to close and a few more days may see the inhabitants of the entire district headed for other climes...

But life went on. This was in the newspaper in October 1917:

A raid was made by District Attorney Geo. W. Smith, Chief of Police Whitsitt and Constable Arthur Devine on the Del Monte Rooming House, in the Krough building, corner of W. Third and Walker streets, last night, and Mrs. Annie Rossi, the woman conducting the place, and another female inmate were arrested and spent the night in the city calaboose.... Justice Hawkins, after a few remarks sentenced her (Mrs. Rossi) to the county jail for six months, and suspended sentence, on conditon that she drop her present mode of life.

———— • ————

During World War II Watsonville was dubbed "Sin City." The following is a portion of an article in the *Battle Cry* magazine issued in 1956:

A hundred miles south of San Francisco, the city of Watsonville is a sleepy agricultural center where apples and strawberries are raised—during the day. At night, under the garish glare of multi-colored neon, this same little city of 13,000 population becomes a sewer with sin for sale, competing with Los Angeles and San Francisco for notoriety in the business of prostitution, gambling and narcotics. The war brought even more prosperity to Watsonville—Fort Ord was built in Monterey and thousands of soldiers, eager for entertainment, especially girls, converged on the area. The gambling tables with fan tan, black jack and the Chinese game of pai gow featured, had an incredible gross. Agriculture became the secondary industry as vice prospered. The Watsonville of today is a comparatively quiet town, but the taxis still transport Fort Ord soldiers to the town and they find their share of prostitutes, and can lose a month's pay at the gaming tables...

In December of 1946 a trial was being held for seven women who were charged with keeping houses of ill fame, six on Union Street and one on Walker Street. During the trial the women testified that they were being charged exorbitant rents, as high as $225 a month. The girls were all from out of town and someone was cashing in on the shady ladies. They were given suspended sentences and ordered out of town.

———— • ————

Tenderloin Woman in Street Battle—'Hatpins to left of them, hair pins to right of them, lunchhooks in all directions, volleyed and thundered'—with apologies to Al Tennyson—but such was the case down on Lower Main street last night near the sobbing Pajaro when Madamoselle Ray Hayes, mistress of a house of joy in the local hoi polloi, came near meeting with her Waterloo at the hands of a "Mrs. John Doe," this name being faked for the reason that to give her true name publicly would be only adding notoriety to a hard working, decent woman. It was too bad that Jack Johnson or "Big Jeff" were absent for they could have grabbed some warm pointers on slugging from these two females, who went at each other hammer and tongs allee samee a brace of cats on a back fence. Madame Hayes started the scrap in the first place. While sitting in the Opera House near "Mrs. Doe," the fairy from the bad lands started to dish out a bunch of insulting junk, which was directed at "Mrs. Doe." "Mrs. Doe" left the show and was trailed down the street by the redlight nymph. When the two principals pulled their freight near a livery stable on Lower Main Street, the Hayes woman was still vomiting forth her deluge of dirty talk. This line of truck became so insulting that "Mrs. Doe" suddenly wheeled upon Mlle. Hayes and then the mixup started. In the first rounds, Mrs. Doe almost put Mlle. Hayes' kisser out of commission, in the second round Mlle. Hayes' lamps were almost put on the blink, in round third, Mlle. Hayes got a lunchhook in the ear-drum, that almost resulted in "taps" being sounded. . . . Anybody that will hurl insults at a decent woman on the street deserves a good, stiff beating, women not excepted, and the person that won't resent an insult with proper blows is either a coward or a fool.

—The *Pajaronian*, December 24, 1909

Chapter Fourteen

And the Rains Came

Special Notice—To the People of the City of Watsonville—Owing to the Water Co.'s flumes being washed away and requiring from two to three days to repair same, you are strictly prohibited from using any water for washing buggies, watering horses, washing sidewalks, or baths, or anything else until further notice; other than cooking and drinking purposes. Anyone caught taking advantage of this, with our shortage of water, will be immediately arrested. Policemen have orders to patrol the streets and arrest anybody violating same. Wash your sidewalks and places of business with the water, as it recedes in the streets.
—P. K. Watters, Mayor of the City of Watsonville,
Evening Pajaronian, March 8, 1911

The flood of 1911 was by no means the first in Watsonville; there had been a number of them over the years starting in 1852 when Watsonville was first laid out. In January of 1890 a storm had been gathering for days and, on January 24, the clouds burst open and a torrent of water fell in a monotonous downpour for two days. Salsipuedes Creek overflowed its banks at several points and the water flowed down to Main Street and to the Pajaro River, flooding much of the east side of town. Then the

The Pajaro Valley Bank, now the site of Wells Fargo Bank, in the flood of 1911.

The Carlton Hotel at Main and Bridge (now Riverside) in 1938.

At Maple Avenue and Main Street, during the flood of 1911. The billiard parlor to the left is now the site of the Fox Theatre. Daly Bros. is on the ground floor of the Porter Building to the right.

Pajaro River broke over its banks and swept down Main Street flooding the plaza, sweeping through yards and spilling into houses and stores. Mud and slimy sediment oozed and settled over dry goods, furniture and carpets, making one big mess.

In the Union, Rodriguez, and Marchant street areas, many residences were flooded and picket fences toppled like toothpicks. The damage was estimated at over $15,000 including the loss of the rich topsoil washed away by the flood. The *Pajaronian* was to note:

The old settlers may dispute as to the comparative size of the flood of 1852, 1862 and 1890 but the latter was certainly far too large for any good use and we believe all our readers are perfectly willing never to experience another siege like that of Saturday night.

The yearly rainfall for 1889-1890 (June to July) was 43.75 inches; the year before it had been 18.42 and the year after it was 18.75; the normal seasonal rain was considered 21.93 inches.

March 8, 1911—"California's people face misfortune with a grin brave enough to face a grizzly bear." By ten o'clock in the morning on March 7, the plaza was covered with flood waters, telephone and telegraph lines were down, and Constable Johnny Corr and Lawrence Sandberg were in their boat, "Search Me," transporting stranded residents. Central Avenue was renamed "Central Rapids" and wading boots were sold out in a few hours with an estimated $2,500 to $3,000 changing hands during the rush.

Mayor Dr. P. K. Watters had a narrow escape while making a professional call on a family on First Street. Two men were rowing him down to the house when an oar got lost in the swirling water and the current upset the craft. The three men climbed up a telephone pole and hung on for an hour before they were finally rescued. Two buggies floated out from Bridge Street (now Riverside) into the middle of Main and snarled up the traffic as they mired in the mud. The newly built Tri-County bridge near Aromas was washed out, creating a loss of over $10,000. At the Morning Star Saloon the water rose to a height of twenty-eight inches and water washed over the stage of the Lyric Theatre to a depth of three or four inches. Out on San Juan Road, young berry plants and trees were washed away, and Nils Dethlefsen reported a loss to his entire berry crop to the tune of $10,000.

No matter what the weather, the Register Pajaronian is delivered! This picture was taken during the 1938 flood, on Main Street near City Hall.

Rodriguez Street in 1911. At lower left is the site of the Wall Street Inn, formerly the Appleton Hotel.

Watsonville gets bathing which shatters all traditions in History of the city. Boats land passengers at Third and Main streets. Water clear to Lake Avenue. The Salsipuedes Creek broke its banks a short distance above the city. There was water, water everywhere and it is also true that there was not a drop to drink, not even in the saloons.
—*Watsonville Register*, March 8, 1911

In 1914, merchants on lower Main Street barricaded their stores with the help of fellow citizens, but the water surged up from the river and into the backs of stores and flooded the town from Beach Street to the river. The sudden rise of the river had been caused by the heavy rains in San Benito County, and, having been forewarned, the people in Watsonville managed to lessen some of the damage. The waters did not reach the plaza; some portions of Maple Avenue received a wetting. The rainfall for the year of 1910-11 was 28.33 inches and for 1913-14 it was 35.90.

But December of 1955 is the one that many local residents remember very well:

Governor Goodwin Knight arrived at Watsonville airport at 10 a.m. Wednesday and immediately set off on a tour of the flood-ravaged area. He was accompanied by state civil defense director Stanley Pierson and his own secretary, Verne Tobia. Led by police chief Frank Osmer who welcomed Knight at the airport, the party toured the Riverside road area along Salsipuedes creek at the point where the levee broke during the height of the flood.
—*Register Pajaronian*, December 28, 1955

The F. A. Wilson home on College Road was carried off by the flood water, the river having reached a height of 33.2 feet. Up in Eureka Canyon the raging Corralitos River cut a swath twenty feet into its west bank, toppling redwood trees and flooding homes, "like Paul Bunyan bowling in the redwoods." Two walls were washed away from the Len Fuller house when a log jam farther up the creek had diverted the water, sending it through the Fuller property.

Drowned in the Pajaro River out Chittenden Pass was J. C. Garcia, section worker for the Southern Pacific Railroad. Another fatality laid to the flood was the death of Amato Rodriguez, who had been evacuated from his home on Lakeview Road and subsequently died of pneumonia at the Watsonville hospital. Thirty-four soldiers arrived on the scene from Fort Ord and were

Satoru Kokka Grocery at 142 Main Street during the flood of 1938, which occurred on February 12.

instrumental in saving the Thurwachter bridge out on Beach Road. They were also used on the Salsipuedes Creek where a new break developed; they helped shore it up.

The measure of a community like the measure of a man, is often the quality of its response to an emergency. Watsonville did herself proud, let it be recorded, during the harrowing hours of last week-end's flood emergency. For enthusiastic response to calls for help, for unselfish effort, you just can't beat the spirit shown by this city's men and women as the Salsipuedes and the Pajaro went on a rampage... It certainly wasn't a normal Christmas week-end. Yet, in view of the response our fellow citizens showed to the needs of others, wasn't it perhaps one of the most Christian Christmases of all!
  —Editorial, Frank Orr, *Register Pajaronian*, December 27, 1955

Looking toward Main Street on Peck Street during the 1938 flood. The plaza is to the right.

Picture Section

This photograph was taken at a teachers' recognition dinner on March 31, 1954. The number following each name indicates the number of years of teaching. Front row, left to right: Helen Hopkins (44), Tacy Dempsey (30), Ellen Jane Cox (48), Clara Dickson (31), Myra Harris (38). Back row, left to right, Dorothy Uren (32), Loretta Allison (42), Leota Flores (35), Sarah Wimmer Nicholson (31), Mae Lord (31), Ruth Benham (30), Martin Thorstensen (30).

Miss Florilla Wickersham, a Watsonville High School teacher, was the first president of the Watsonville Woman's Club, in 1899.

The library in the IOOF reading room in the 1890s. Belle Jenkins, the librarian, worked five days a week, afternoons and evenings, for twenty dollars a month.

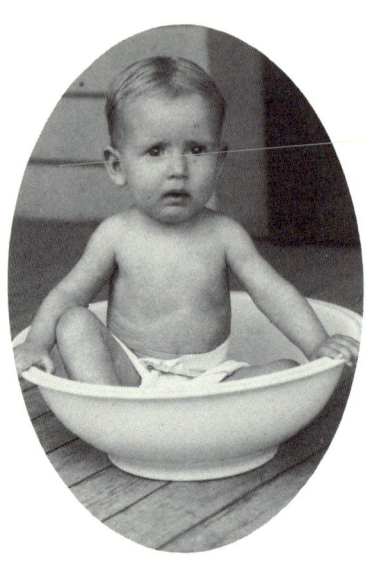

Ruth Turner, long-time employee at Ford's, at the age of six months.

St. Patrick's Church on upper Main Street was built in 1903 for $50,000. William H. Weeks was the architect. Photograph by Elizabeth McBride-Smith.

Former stage stop on old Mt. Madonna Road was purchased by the Marshall family in 1879 and converted into a home. It was torn down when a new home was built. This is where Charley Parkhurst stopped his stage on the San Juan route. Standing in front of the house are, from left to right, Ada, Rose, Manuel, and Anna Marshall.

This collection of photographs of prominent members of El Pajaro Parlor, No. 35, Native Daughters of the Golden West, is dated 1892. 1. Miss Eda Chalmers; 2. Mrs. Frank Johnson; 3. Miss Hattie Cox; 4. Miss May Martin; 5. Mrs. Cora Harvey; 6. Mrs. Flora Billings; 7. Miss Eva Leland; 8. Miss Christine Struve; 9. Miss Bertha Lewis; 10. Mrs. I. H. Chapin; 11. Miss Sarah Cox; 12. Mrs. Josie Roache French; 13. Mrs. J. J. Malcolm; 14. Mrs. Mary Stuart; 15. Miss Esther Malcolm.

Main Street in Watsonville in 1875, looking south towards the bridge. On the left is the Mansion House Hotel and behind it the plaza. On the right are Fred Werner's boot and shoe shop, Ford and Sanborn, Cooper House, Cooper Emporium, and the Stoesser Building.

Jack Novcich in his cigar store at 424 Main Street in the 1940s. He had a ten-year lease at thirty-two dollars a month, and had the first neon sign in town in front of his store. The cigar stand originally had three card tables in the back portion. Jack moved into this part of the Mansion House in 1914.

Southern Pacific Passenger Depot on Walker Street, across from the Railroad Exchange Hotel.

Buick in front of the Trafton house, now the site of Watsonville High School on East Beach Street. The Warren Porter home in the background is now owned by Mrs. Katharine Pista.

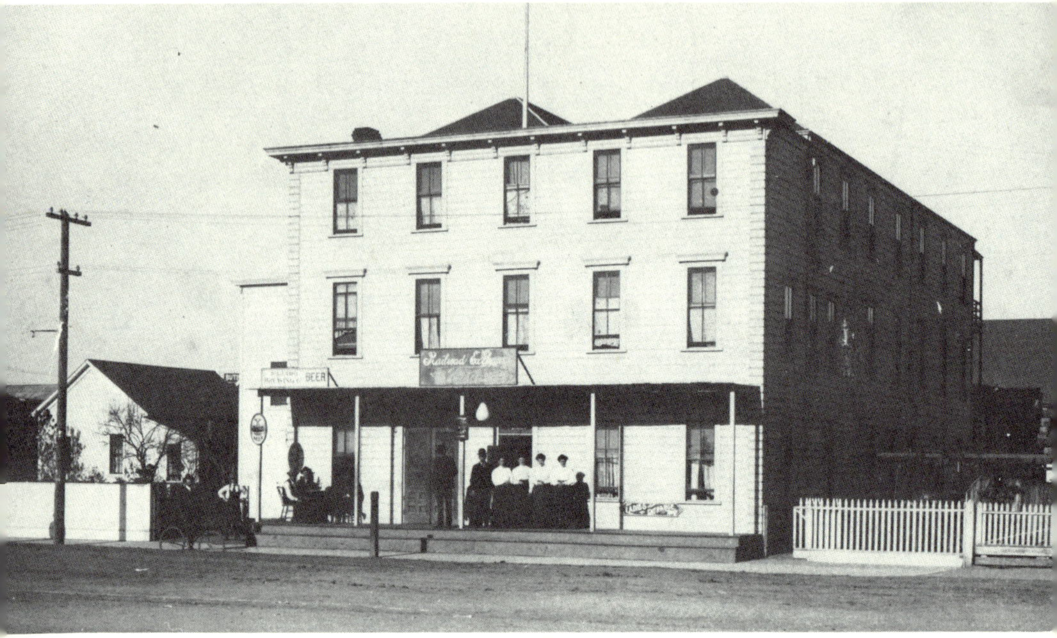

Railroad Exchange Hotel at 316 Walker Street was built in 1893 by George Strazicich. The sign on the lower right of the building says "Ladies Entrance."

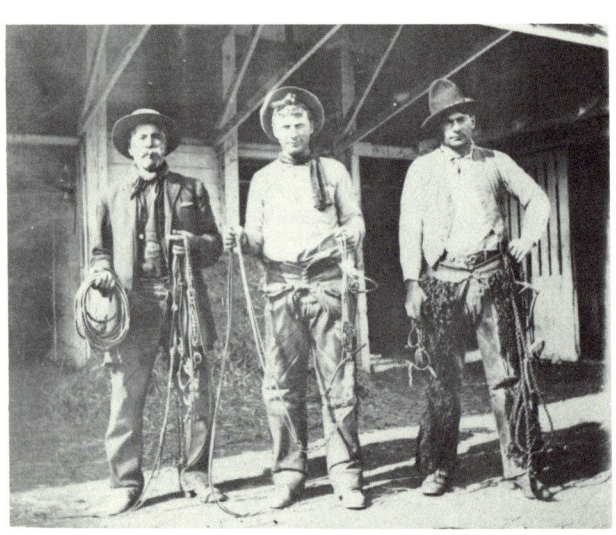

Necrasco Castro is on the left and Doc Florence Arano on the right. The name of the man in the middle is unknown.

Funeral Notice

Friends and acquaintances are respectfully invited to attend the Funeral of the late

JULIUS LEE

(A native of Connecticut, aged 80 years, 11 months and 3 days. Died at Watsonville, Cal., March 28, 1910.)

Which will take place from the Methodist Church, on

Wednesday, March 30 1910,
At 10:00 o'clock, a. m.

Remains will be taken to Cypress Lawn Cemetery on noon train, for cremation.

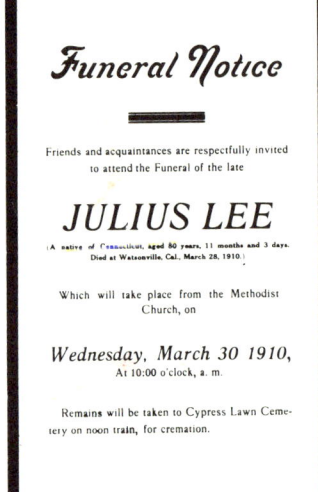

The graduation class of Carrolton School, June 1901. Standing are Harry Rowe and Alice Reid, the teacher. Seated are Mabel Rowe and Julia Daly.

Company L entraining at the Watsonville depot on June 23, 1916.

Main and West Lake, the site of the Resetar Hotel, built in 1927. The building on the corner was moved to Rodriguez Street and was torn down in the early 1970s. The Mundhenk Building to the far left is now the site of Woolworth's.

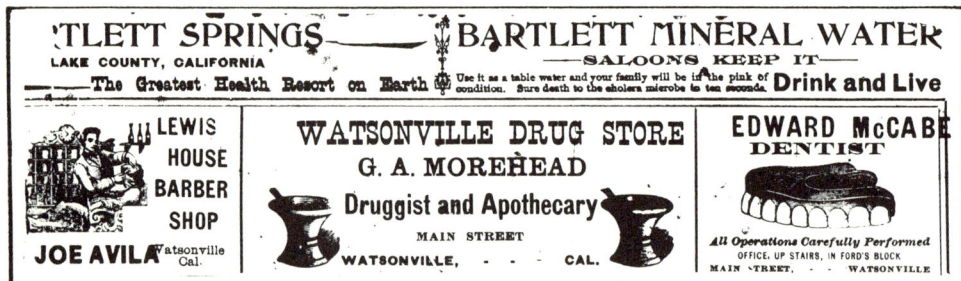

Advertisements dated 1895.

Old fashioned apple spraying outfit in front of Pajaro Valley Construction Railroad Office and Freight Depot, at the present site of the Watsonville Exchange.

This house, which was the home of Phillip Adam Martin, was torn down in 1947 and a new one was constructed on the site in 1950 by his grandson, Henry A. Martin. The present address is 479 Riverside Road. Phillip Adam Martin was a native of Baden, Germany who came to California in 1856 and settled in the Pajaro Valley in 1868.

Ford's delivery truck at the turn of the century, driven by Chris Struve. The case in front contains two cans of Pearl Oil, produced by the Standard Oil Company for family use.

Mundhenk's Bakery at 507 Main Street, about 1894. Later it was the Golden Crust Bakery.

Appendix

CITY OFFICIALS - 1980

MAYOR
William "Bill" Johnston

COUNCIL MEMBERS
Vido T. Deretich
Jean M. McNeil
Elizabeth (Betty) Murphy
Frank Osmer
Charles A. Palmtag
Ann M. Soldo

City Manager	James W. Buell
City Attorney	Donald Haile
City Clerk	Dorothy Bennett
Fire Chief	Vern Hamilton
Police Chief	Al Williams
Library Director	Seely Sumpf
Planning Director	Bob Ellenwood
Public Works Director	John Cooper
Recreation Director	Pat Donohue
Building Official	Dick Jones
Administrative Services Director	John Radin

References

NEWSPAPERS
Alta California, San Francisco, California
Evening Pajaronian, Watsonville, California
Monterey Sentinel, Monterey, California
Pacific Coast Commerical Record: Pajaro Valley Edition. San Francisco, January 10, 1890.
Pacific Sentinel, Santa Cruz, California
The Pajaronian, Watsonville, California
Register-Pajaronian, Watsonville, California
Salinas Daily Index, Salinas, California

BOOKS
Abajian, James. 1977. *Blacks in Selected Newspapers and Other Sources.* Boston: G. K. Hall.
Atkinson, Fred W. 1934. *100 Years in the Pajaro Valley.*
Beautiful Santa Cruz County. 1896. San Francisco: H. S. Crocker Company.
Commercial Encyclopedia of the Pacific Southwest. 1915. Oakland, California: Ellis A. Davis.
Illustrations of Santa Cruz County. 1879. San Francisco: Wallace W. Elliott & Co.
Halliwell, Leslie. 1978. *The Filmgoer's Companion*, Sixth Edition.
Harrison, E. S. 1892. *History of Santa Cruz County.* San Francisco: Pacific Press Publishing Co.

OTHER SOURCES
Watsonville City Directories, 1898 through 1950
Documents in the Recorder's Office, Santa Cruz County Courthouse, Santa Cruz, California.
Documents in the Probate Department, Santa Cruz County Courthouse, Santa Cruz, California.
Maps, memoirs, diaries, genealogies, scrapbooks, picture albums, school programs, school yearbooks, oral histories, census records.
William Volck Memorial Museum, 261 East Beach Street, Watsonville, California 95076.

Index
By Sam Stark

Alaga Brothers, 75
Albert, Kenneth, 33
Albright (Police Chief), 88
Albright, Etta, 34
Albright, Jane, 34
Albright, Joseph, 34
Albright, Josephine, 34
Albright, May, 34
Albright, Myrtle, 34
Albright, Thomas, 34-*36*
Albright, William, 34
Aldridge, Frank, 92-93
Alexander and Billings, xi
Alexander and Sons, 91
Alford, H. N., 52
Alford, T. N., 52
Algar, Margaret S., 60
Allison, Ethel, 52
Allison, Loretta, *135*
Alvarado, Governor, xi
Amesti School District, 12, 52, 60
Amesti, Jose, 4
Amesti School, 52
Amos, Walter Lewis, 33
Anderson, Edna E., 60
Andrews, P. M., 98
Andrishevich and Vucicevich, 75
Angel Face (musical), 38
Anzar, Juan Miguel, 4
Appleton Garage, *85*
Appleton Hotel, 70
Appleton Investment Company, 41, 45
Appleton Theatre, 41-42, *43*, 45, 47
Arano, "Doc" Florence, *140*
Arano, John and Modesto, 122
Archie, John ("Kilwee"), *33*
Aromas School, *55*
Aston, Eva, 35
Ashton, John C., 52, 68
Ashton, Joseph, 66
Avancina, Mrs. Mary W., 60
Avila, Joe, 142

Bachelder, C. S., 110
Backus, Mrs. S. W., 32
Bailey, Guy L., 88
Baker, C. H., 41, 78
Bank of Watsonville, 118, 120
Barber, Adam, 98
Barney; Ford (Charles) and, 9
Battinich Company, 75
Baxter, J. A., 108-109
Baxter, J. W., 78
Beach Road School, 57-58

Beck, A. P., 63
Beck, Andy, 122
Beck, Thomas, 115
Beebe, Dr. Charles, 111
Beilby, Claude, *54*
Beilby, Leroy, *54*
Benham, Ruth, *135*
Bergman, Helen Watters, 86
Billings; Alexander and, xi
Billings, Mrs. Flora, *137*
Bixby, A. L., 110
Black Cat (apple), 76
Blackburn home, 116
Blackburn, J. A., 117
Blair, James, 4
Blohm, Archie, 112
Blohm, Mrs. H. F., 103
Bloomer Baseball Club, 36
Bockius, Godfrey, xi
Bodfish Canyon Road, 24
Boin, Charles, *80*
Bonde, Martin, 52
Bonnet, Mr. and Mrs. D'Arcy, 69
Bradbury, F. R., 63
Brassel, H. P., 68
Brassel, Helen, 60
Braycovich, J. P., and Company, 75
Brennan, James, xii, 13
Brennan's landing, xii
Brewington block, 41
Brewington, George, 122
Briggs, Frank, 122
Broadis, Amanda, 122
Broadis, Ellen, 122
Broadis, Ellen Maria, 122-123
Broadis, Harriet, 122
Broadis Hill, 122
Broadis, James, *120*-123
Broadis, James, Jr., 122-123
Broadis, Mabel, 122
Broadis, Priscilla, 122-123
Broadis, Tel, 122-123
Brown's Valley School, 60
Buchanan, P. G., xii
Burgoin, William, 99
Burke, Billie, *38*, 41
Burland Brothers, 91, 122
Burton, Sumner, 39
Butman, Nellie, 93
Butterfield, Beatrice, *103*
Butterfield, Bernice, *103*
Butterfield, Dr. Charles, 17, *102*, *103*, 104
Butterfield, Dorothy, *103*
Butterfield, Mr. and Mrs. Joseph, 103
Butterfield, Marian, *103*

147

Caddy, Mary, 60
Cadwalader family, 52
Calabasas School, 54, 60
California Fruit Packing Company, 75
California Restaurant, 32, 100
California Theatre, 45, 46, 47-48
Callaghan Playground, 122
Camp Goodall, 15
Camp McQuaide, 28, 29
Cano, Gil (constable), 93
Capitanich, J. C., 75
Carey, Lemmie, 54
Carey, May, 54
Carlton Hotel, 130
Carlton School, 60
Carr, Hon. Jesse D., xii, 13
Carroll, Seneca, 53
Carrolton School, 54, 57, 141
Carrolton School District, 53
Carter, Charles, xi
Casa Materna; La, 6
Casserly School, 60
Cassin, Bella, 57
Castro, Antonio, 4
Castro, Guadalupe, 4
Castro, Joaquin, 4
Castro, Nevrasco, 140
Cathers, James, 53
Centre Theatre, 49
Century Garage, 35-36, 87
Chaballa, Romaldo, 91
Chalmers, Alex, 15, 52
Chalmers, Eda, 137
Chapin, Mrs. I. H., 137
Chaplin, Charles, 42
Chapman, H. L., 76
Chittenden, Nathaniel W., 21, 23
Chittenden Pass, 21, 22, 74, 81, 133
Chittenden Road, 21, 22, 25
Chittenden Springs, 25-27
Chittenden, Talman, 23, 26
Clark and Clark, 70
Clausen, Carrie M., 93, 94, 95
Cleveland, Lin, 121
Cloud, A. D., 53
Clough, D. M., 53
Clough, Johanna, 57
Clough, Julia, 57
Coleman, S. Waldo, 41
College Lake, 112
Company L (U.S. Army), 141
Cooper block, 80, 108
Cooper Emporium, 138
Cooper, Ernest, 122
Cooper house, 12, 19, 138
Cooper, Captain Juan, 1
Copeland, J. D., 75
Copriviza and Gera, 75
Copriviza, George, 78
Cornell, Myrtle, 29

Cornell Tractor Company, 88
Corr, Johnny, 100, 131
Corralitos Fruit Growers, Inc., 76, 79
Corralitos School, 60
Cottrell, Charles, 80
Courter, H. F., 53
Covell, John, 36
Coward, Kate, 57
Coward, Maggie, 57
Cowles, Herbert, 52
Cox, A. W., 105
Cox, Annie, 52
Cox, Arnie, 109
Cox, Ellen Jane, 135
Cox, Gilbert, 59
Cox, Hattie, 137
Cox, L. P., 123
Cox, Leslie, 59
Cox, Lyman, 85
Cox, Sarah, 137
Craighead, Eula, 60
Croton, S.S., 10
Cumming, Bill, 21
Cupid, Al, 109, 122
Cutler, Edna, 55
Cutter, J. B., 78

Daley and Quinn Brothers Meat Market, 96
Daly Brothers Store, 92, 97, 130
Daly, Denis Joseph, 97
Daly, Denis, Jr., 97
Daly, Julia, 141
Daly, Pat, 97
Daras, Jean, 125
Davidson, Mamie, 92
de Hara, Francisco, 4
de Leon, Vicenta, 1, 5
Del Monte Rooming House, 126-127
Dempsey, Tacy, 135
Dethlefsen, Nils, 131
Dethlefsen, Andrew, 52
Devine, Arthur, 32, 122, 126
Devine, Tom, 122
Dewey Brand (apple), 72
Dibble, P. K., 59
Dickson, Clara, 135
Diehm's, 97
Dondero block, 100
Dot Theatre, 41
Douglas, Clarence, 33
Douglas, H. B., 29, 52
Downey, M. J., 68
Downing (Marshal), 125
Downing, William, 112
Driscoll, Raymond, 57

Earl Fruit Company, 74, 75, 87
East Lake Village Shopping Center, 102
Eaton, Bessie, 54

Eaton, Charley, *54*
Eaton, Hazel, *54*
Eaton, Roy, 99
Eaton, Walter, *54*
Eclipse Livery Stable, 92, 98
Edward, George, *33*
Edward, George, Sr., *33*
Edwin, Arthur (Eddie), *33*
Eiggia, John, 75
El Dorado Meat Market, 91
El Pajaro Springs, 25, *26*, 27, 44
El Pajaro Theatre Company, 45, 48
Elite Chop House, 91
Elmer, Richard, *33*
Emkay Candy Factory, 91
Enemark, James, 122
Erickson, Dorothy, 25, 27
Erickson, Robert, 27
Eureka School, 50, 60
Evans, Doug, 100

Farm and Forest Realty Company, 101
Faustino, A., 123
Felix, Anna, 45
Fergoda, L., 89
Ferndale School, 51, 60
Fetzman, Vincent A., 98
Fields, W. C., *43*
Fletcher, Henry S., 119, *120*, 122
Flores, Leota, *135*
Fogg, Bill, xi
Foltz, W. S., 87
Foote, Harold and Lou, 99
Ford, Charles, 9-20, *11*, 70, 92, 122
Ford (Charles) Company, *10*, 11, *12*, *14-17*, 18-20, 29, 47, 63, 95, *109*, 136, 143
Ford (Charles) and Barney, 9
Ford (Charles) and Sanborn (Lucius) Company, xi, *14*, 31-32, *138*
Forrester, Lynden, 52
Fox Theatre, *44*, *46*, 47-48, 130
Fox West Coast Theatres, 47
French, Mrs. Josie Roache, *137*
Frondsen, Eddie, *54*
Frondsen, Ellen, *54*
Fruitvale School, 60
Frykland, Ranghild, 60
Fuller, Len, 133

Gaddie, Felix Grundy, 68
Garcia, J. C., 133
Gardner, John, 78
George, Hattie, *74*
Gianotti, Edythe, 45
Gilman, Dr. Philip, Jr., 119
Gilman, Mrs. Philip, Jr., 114-115, 119
Gilroy Hot Springs, 25
Gleason, Walter, 112
Golden Crust Bakery, 144
Golden Sheaf Flouring Mill, 92

Goodale, Everett, 78-79
Gospodnetich, Kosmos, 75
Gotsch, Dr. Otto H., 98
Grace School, 58
Graves, Matt, 112
Green, Nat, 123
Green Valley School District, 53, 60
Gregory, Durell S., 1-3
Grimes, Miss (teacher), 50
Grizich, Matthew, 75
Grul, William, 64
Guild Hall, 52
Guioco delle Boccie, 92
Gukan, Peter and Company, 75
Gulick, W. D., 87
Gurash and Stolich, 75

Hall, Archie, 99
Hall, James A., 98
Harris, Florence, 60
Harris, Myra, *135*
Hartnell Junior College, 31
Harvey, Cora, *137*
Haskin, Jack and Stella, 101
Hawkins (Justice), 127
Hawkins and Peckham, 66
Hayes, Ray, 127-128
Hazel Dell School, 56, 60
Hecker, Henry, 24
Hecker Pass, 24
Henry, Thomas (Harry), *33*
Hernandez, Felipe, 4
Hildreth block, 39, *42*, 116
Hildreth Building, 45
Hildreth, Sol, 39-40
Hill, C. Keith, 53
Hill, J. Bryant, xii, 122
Hill School, 60
His Little Sister (play), 40
Hobbs, W. H., 53
Holohan, James, 52
Hop Chan Apple Evaporating Co., 78
Hopkins, Helen, *135*
Hopkins, Irene, *74*
Horgan, Julia, 52
Horgan, T. J., 67
Hosgland (constable), 125
Howard, Kate, 57
Hoyt, Lizzie, *54*
Hrepich, Anna, 45
Hungry Hollow School, *59*
Hushbeck, Charles, 112
Hyde Park Theatre, 49

Independent Creamery, 99
Independent Order of Odd Fellows Hall, 103, *135*
Ingham, James, 65, 68, 70
Irish, Claude, *18*
Ivoncovich, Vojvodich and Company, 75

Jackson, Mrs. Adele, 118
Jackson, H. Nelson, 86
Jackson, Henry, xii
James, Harry, 40
Japanese Theatre, 40, 49
Jazz Singer, The (film), 47
Jenkins, Belle, *135*
Jerome, F. S., 78
Jerry (play), 41
Jessen, George, 105
Jewett, Dr. S., 98
Jimeno, Manuel, 4
Joe's (Joseph Pitoja) Saloon, 92
Johnson, Mrs. Fannie, 56
Johnson, Mrs. Frank, *137*
Johnson, Harry, 99
Johnson, Mrs. Israel ("Mam-Mam"), 68
Johnson, Rev. J. G., xii
Johnstone, Lavisa, 45
Jones Brothers, 77-78
Jones Garage, 85
Jones, J. H. W., 52
Jones, Josephine, 45
Jones, Maude, 53
Joseph, Frank, *56*
Joseph, Mary, *56*
Joy, A. E., 86
Joy, Florence, 92
Judd, A. N., 61

Kalich Building, 41
Kane, Styleta, 60
Kee, Chong Tong, 77
Kelley, Rev. D. O., 58
Kelly, Mrs. Edward J., 34
Kelly, Patrick, 116
Kelly-Thompson family, 57, 61, 120
Kennedy, Thomas, 92
Kennedy, William H., 98
Kerr, Julia, 57
Kersham, John, 39
Kidder, Louise, 57
Kilburn, F. A., 20
Kimmel, Ed, 100
Kitchen, Frank, 101
Knight, Governor Goodwin, 133
Knowlton, Owen T., 99
Kray, John and Company, 75
Kreiger Vinegar Company, 75, 78
Krogh, A. A., 69
Krough Building, 126
Krough, F. P., 41
Kukuliza, M., and Company, 75

La Petite Theatre, 38-40, 42, 44
Langley, C. F., 78, 123
Langley, Charles, 41
Lansburgh, G. Albert, 45
Lara, Robert, 47
Larkin Valley School, 55

Las Manzanitas School, 60
Lasher, William, 112
Lawn, Dr. A. Ray, 66
Leask, Mrs. Samuel (nee Clara Johnson), 56, 68
Lee, Elmore, 35, 80
Lee, Julius, 140
Lee, William, 33
Leeson, John, 100
Leland, Eva, *137*
Leland, Mrs. George, 34
Lenzen, Jacob, 17
Lettunich Building, xi, 97
Lettunich, E. B., 76
Lettunich, M. N., 71-72, 76, 78, 87
Lettunich, Mateo, 68, 71-72, 87
Lewis and Son, 91
Lewis, A., and Company, 24, 95
Lewis, Bertha, *137*
Lewis block, 61
Lewis House Barber Shop, 142
Limburgh, Sam, 34
Linda (strawberry), 118
Lindley School District, 51-52
Linscott, James A., 81, 83, 88
Logan, C., 98
Loma Fruit Company, 76
Loma Prieta Mill, 63
Longley, Daisy, 17
Lopes, Allen, 21
Lopes, Louis, *21*
Lord, Mae, *135*
Love's Wireless (song), 104
Lucich and Gordon, 76
Lyric Theatre, 40
Lyric (New) Theatre, 41-42, 44, 131

McBride-Smith, Elizabeth, 136
McCabe, Edward, 142
McClean, Louie, *109*
McDermott, Bill, xi
McDonald and Sons, 76
McDougal, Fred A., 4
McDowell Printing Service, 100
McEven, J. H., 53
McGhee, Mrs. Fannie, 58
McGowan, William, 52
McGrath, W. J., 78
McIntyre, V. F., 111
McLean's Blacksmith Shop, 101
McLellan, Bernice, 60
McQuaide, Major Joseph P., 29
McSherry, Gladys Tuttle, 66

MacDonald and Sons, 73
Mackrell, Charles, 82, 86
Maher, D. F., 98
Mahlgren, E., 110
Main Street, *83, 85, 90, 124, 138*
Malcolm, Esther, *137*

150

Malcolm, Mrs. J. J., *137*
Mann, Edith, 57
Mann, Edna, 57
Mann, Gladys, *54*
Mansion House Hotel, 23, *138*
Maple Avenue, *67*
March, Marjorie, 60
Marcus, Jennie, 57
Mariposa Building and Saloon, 92
Marisch, Frank, 87
Markowitz Brothers, 45
Marshall, Ada, *136*
Marshall, Anna, *136*
Marshall family, 136
Marshall, Manuel, *136*
Marshall, Rose, *136*
Martel, A. F., 25-26
Martin Brothers, 76
Martin, Edward, 117
Martin, Ella A., 60
Martin, George P., 61, 68, 70, 108-109
Martin, Henry A., 143
Martin, May, *137*
Martin, Phillip Adam, 143
Mauk, Ed, 110
Mello, Angelino, 51
Mello, Henry, 34
Menasco, George Tuttle, 19, 31
Menasco, James Sidney, 15, 19
Menasco, Sidney T., *18*-19
Mengol, Peter, 76
Merchant and Hagerty, 101
Miljanich, J., and Company, 76
Milks, Jerome, 122
Miller, Jim and Georgia, 70
Miller, "Speed," 81
Ming, Jan, 78
Miovich, J. F., and Company, 76
Mitchell, Thomas, xi
Monarch Vinegar Company, 77
Monterey Bay Academy, 28-29
Monterey County Court House, Salinas, 119
Monterey Savings and Loan, 108
Moon, A. H., 20
Morehead, G. A., 142
Moreland Notre Dame Academy, 61
Morey, A. A., 15
Morning Star Saloon, 131
Morse, Charles, 4
Morse, Milton J., 76
Mount Madonna, 24-25
Mundhenk Building, *142*
Mundhenk's Bakery, *144*
Mustol, S. J., 104
Muybridge, E. J., 116

Native Daughters of the Golden West, 95, *137*
Nebraska Hotel, 12

Newman, A., 68, 107
Nicholson, Sarah Wimmer, *54, 135*
Nickelodian, 39
"Nigger Hill," 122
Nistetter, Gus, 112
Novacovich and Stolich, 76
Novacovich, Stork, 34
Novcich, Jack, *138*

Oak Grove School District, 53
Odd Fellow's Building, 93
Office Supply Company, 101
Old Corner Saloon, 100-101
Oldfield, Barney, 86
Oliver, Frank E., 89
Oliver Realty Company, 66
Ordish, Joseph, 66
Orr, Frank, 134
Osborn family, 68
Osmer, Frank, 133
Ostrander (Alderman), 126
Ostrander, John, 70
Our Gang (comedies), 47
Owl Recreation Parlor, 102
Owsley, B. F., 63

Pacheco, Perfecto (Senora Sebastian Rodriguez), 1, 5
Pacific Evaporating Company, 76, 78
Pacific Exchange Hotel, xi
Pajaro Dunes South, 15
Pajaro Landing, 15
Pajaro Packing Company, 76, 78
Pajaro School, *50*
Pajaro Theatre, 47
Pajaro Valley Bank, *130*
Pajaro Valley Construction, *142*
Pajaro Valley Fair Association, 118
Pajaro Valley Fruit Growers, 76
Pajaro Valley Nursery, *117*-118
Pajaro Valley Pool Room, 102
Pajaro Valley Schools, 60
Pajaro Valley Vinegar Company, 77
Pajaro Wheel Club, 105, 108, 111
Palmtag, Charles A., 105-*106*
Palmtag, Ray, 99
Paraiso Hot Springs, 15, 25
Pardee, George C., 83
Parker, Harry, 119
Parkhurst, Charley, 136
Paulsen, Anna, 60
Pecarovich, M., and Company, 76
Peck block, 102, 103, 108, 111
Peckham and Judd, 118
Peckham, H. A., 123
Peckham, H. C., 91, 112
Pekoch, S., and Company, 76
Pena and Hall's Clothing Store, *80*, 108
Pena, Fred, 32-33
Pep Creamery, *90*, 99-100

Peralto, Mary, 125
Perry and Hrepich, 76
Peters, Mr. and Mrs. Frank, 97
Peterson's Point, 112
Pfingst, Edward, 45
Phillips, Eddie, 102
Pico, Jose Delores, 4
Pierce Cyclery, *110*
Pierson, T. C., 67
Pinto Lake, 116
Pioneer Cemetery, 13
Pioneer Cyclery, 110
Pippin Baseball Team, 34-35
Pippin Theatre, 42, 44
Piratsky, James, 37-*38*, 40-41
Piratsky, Mrs. James, 38-41
Piroja, Joseph, 92
Pista, J., and Company, 77
Pista, Mrs. Katharine, 139
Pleasant Valley School, *59*
Porter Building, 97, *130*
Porter, John T., 61
Porter, Warren, 61, 139
Portola, Gaspar de, 6
Posa, La, 5
Pulich, L., and Company, 77

Quality First (apple), 75
Quinn Brothers, 122
Quong Sung Lung Company, 78

Radcliff School, 29
Radcliff, W. R., 78
Radone, Fred, 39
Radovan, Frank, 77
Railroad Exchange Hotel, 139-*140*
Railroad Office, *142*
Railroad School, 57, 60-61
Ramsey, Dr. W. J. C., 98
Rancho Bolsa de San Cayetano, 4
Rancho Bolsa del los Rodriguez, 1, 3
Rancho Bolsa del Rio del Pajaro, 1, 4-5, 7
Rancho Canada de Salsipuedes, 4
Rancho de la Ballena, 5, 7
Rancho La Lagune de Las Calabasas, 4
Rancho Las Aromitas y Las Aguas Calientes, 4
Rancho Los Corralitos, 4
Rancho San Andres, 4
Rancho Vega del Rio del Pajaro, 4
Raphael, Otto, 123
Rappe, Carl, 91, 123
Rasco's, 85
Raymond, Bonita, 45
Raymond, Dorita, 45
Reagan, Frank, 57
Reckoning of the Clutching Hand (film serial), 49
Red Anchor (apple), 75

Redman, Christy, 107
Redman, James, 58
Redwood School, 60
Reid, Alice, *59*, *141*
Rendezvous Billiard Parlor, 39
Resetar, Balich and Company, 77
Resetar Hotel, *142*
Rider, Frank, 69
Rilovich and Company, 77
Roache School, *55*, 60
Roache, William, 123
Robinson, F. E., 111
Rodeo Theatre, 49
Rodgers, Carroll, 78
Rodgers, Dan, 123
Rodgers, Mrs. Esther, 116
Rodgers, Frank, 41
Rodgers, James, 116
Rodgers, Ruth, 60
Rodonich, N., and Company, 77
Rodriguez, Alejandro, 1, 4
Rodriguez, Amato, 133
Rodriguez, Antonio, 5
Rodriguez, Bernabela, 5, 7
Rodriguez, Carmen, 5, 7
Rodriguez, Deciderio, 5, 7
Rodriguez, Facundo, 2-3
Rodriguez, Jacinto, 5, 7
Rodriguez, Jose Antonio, 1, 5, 7
Rodriguez, Ma. Antonio, 5, 7
Rodriguez, Pedro, 5, 7
Rodriguez, Pete, 122
Rodriguez, Rafaila, 5, 7
Rodriguez, Ramona, 5, 7
Rodriguez, Sebastian, 1-5, 7-8
Rodriguez, Solano, 5, 7
Rodriguez, Teresa, 5, 7
Rohrback, Judge Daniel Webster, 93
Rohrback Store, *93*
Ross, Onie, 58
Rowan, Tommy, 34
Rowe, Edna, 60
Rowe, Harry, *141*
Rowe, Mabel, *141*
Rowe, Marie O., 60
Rowe, Shirley, *54*
Rowe, Willie, *54*
Rubas, Dizzy, 34
Rudasill, Mrs. Ouida, 60
Ruppert, Mrs. F. R. (Hazel), 118-119

Saint Francis Springs, 25-26
Saint Patrick's Church, 116, *136*
Salazar, Ralph, 47
Salinas High School, 31
Salinas, S.S., xii
Salsipuedes School District, 53
San Andreas School, 60
San Jose State University, 31
San Monte Fruit Company, 72, 75, 77

Sanborn, Lucius, xi, 13, 15, 19, 31-32, 122
Sanborn, Lucius W., 32
Sanborn, Nellie, 32
Sanchez, Don Jose, 123
Sandberg, Lawrence, 131
Santa Clara University, 29
Sassilo Brothers, 77
Satoru Kokka Grocery, *134*
Schafer, Lena, 60
Schroeder, Henry, 58
Scott, Carrie, 32
Scott, R. J., xi
Scott's Boarding House, 13
Scurich, A. A., and Company, 77
Scurich Brothers, 77
Scurich, J., and Company, 77
Scurich, Stephen, 123
Secondo Brothers, 77
Seevers, Clay W., 98
Seitz, J. A., *110*
Service Printers, 100
Sheehy, James, 68, 87, 91
Sheehy, Jerry, 52
Sheehy, Philip, 41
Short, Malinda, 116
Shultz, F. A., 36
Sibole, Charles, *80*
Silliman, Carl, 57
Silliman family, 57
Simmon, Robert, 21, 23
Simpson and Hack Packing Plant, 71, *76*
Simpson, Frank Fruit Company, 77
Simunovich, Jasper, 77
Skillicorn Baseball Team, 33-34
Skillicorn, Eddie, 33-34
Skillicorn, Elmer, 34
Skillicorn, George "Pop," 34
Smith, George W., 126
Snyder, Albert, 22
Snyder, Elmer, 57
Southern Pacific Depot, *139*
Southworth, Mrs. M. P., 58
Sparks, Margaret, 55
Speas Company, 77
Speegle, Maggie, 57
Spencer, Bert and Kay, 53
Spreckels Sugar Factory, 17, 66-67
Springfield School District, 58
Stanton, Mr. and Mrs. Ralph, 119
Staples, Blossom, 51
Starlite Drive-In Theatre, 49
State Theatre, *43*, 47
Steglich, Frieda, *92*
Steinhauser and Eaton Drug Store, *90*, 96, 99
Steinhauser, Elliott, 99, 101
Stoesser Building, 61, 116, *138*
Stoesser, Otto, 1, 13, 93
Stoesser, Otto D., 41

Stolich Brothers, 77
Storm, Minnie, *92*
Stow, Willie, 57
Strazicich, Andrew, *100*
Strazicich, George, 140
Strazicich, Nick, *92*
Struve, Chris, *143*
Struve, Christine, *137*
Struve, Jim, 122
Stuart, Mrs. Mary, *137*
Sudden, Captain, 117
Sudden tract, 113, 117
Sully, George, Jr., 26
Sunblest (apple), 75
Swank, Judge, 125
Sweeny, J. W., xii
Sylva, Mary, 59

T & D (Turner and Dahnken) Theatre, Salinas, 38, 41
T & D Theatre, Watsonville, *43*-45, 47
Tassajara Hot Springs, 25
Tavares, Joseph and Mary, 51
Taylor, Theodore and Mary, 101
Tenny, H. M., 78
Thompson, Chris, 36
Thompson, Maggie, 57
Thompson, Russell, 57
Thorstensen, Martin, *135*
Thurwachter, Louise, 57-58
To Kill A Man (play), 40
Trabing, Louis, 112
Trafton, Sheriff Howard, 32, 111
Trafton, John, 41
Trafton, William A., 67, 123
Travers, M. A., Company, 77
Tubbs Fruit Company, Salinas, 38
Tullock, J. W., 78
Tupper, Mrs. Flora B., 60
Turner and Dahnken, 44
Turner, Ruth, *136*
Tuttle, Adele, 66
Tuttle, Daniel, 65
Tuttle, Edna, 19
Tuttle, Mrs. Frank, 34
Tuttle, George, 106
Tuttle, Gladys, 66
Tuttle, H. D., 19
Tuttle, I. H., 110
Tuttle, Ione, 110
Tuttle, Lee, 66
Tuttle, Mabel, 66
Tuttle, Mary, 19
Tuttle, Morris Burns, 61-66
Tuttle, Mrs. Morris Burns (nee Mary Ingles), 65-66
Tuttle, Owen, xii, 65-66
Tuttle, Victor, 19, 108, 110
Tuttle, Warren, 66, 119
Tyler, Mrs. Mary Y., 60

Underwood, Mr. and Mrs., 52
Unique Theatre, 37
United Apple Growers, 77
United States Army. See Company L
Universal City, California, 43
Uren, Dorothy, 135

Valenzuela, Sacramento, xi
Vallejo, Ignacio, 4
Vallejo, Ignacio Vicente Ferrar, 6
Vallejo, Jose de Jesus, 4
Valley National Bank, 13
Valley Sport Shop, 109
Van Doren, William, 59
Vaughan, H. W., 36
Veterans Memorial Building, 124
Vidak, Luke, 102
Vlasich, P., and Company, 77
Volck (William) Museum, 52
Vyeda, Tony, 80

Walker, Mrs. James, 118
Wall Street Inn, 132
Wallace (Justice), 126
Waters, Adele, 118
Waters, Hazel, 118
Waters, James, 24, 113, *114*, 115-119
Waters, Lola, 118
Waters, Malinda Short, *114*, 116, 119
Waters subdivision, 119
Waters, William, 118-*119*
Waters, Willie, 118
Watson, Judge John Howard, 1-3, 13
Watsonville Apple Distributors, 78
Watsonville Canning Company, 78
Watsonville Cider and Vinegar Company, 77
Watsonville Cyclery, 111
Watsonville Drug Store, 99, 142
Watsonville Exchange, 142
Watsonville Fire Station, 28-*30*, 116
Watsonville Garage, 85, 88
Watsonville Heights, 123
Watsonville High School, 139
Watsonville Oil Company, 74
Watsonville Opera House, 37, 39, 41, *103*

Watsonville Plaza, 2, *134*, *138*
Watsonville Realty Company, 123
Watt, James, 123
Watters, Dr. P. K., 61, 86-87, 129, 131
Weeks, Jean, 99
Weeks, William H., 19, 29, 41, 53, 55, 57-58, 61, *63*-65, 68, 70, 75-76, 89, 110, 119, 136
Wells Fargo Bank, 130
Werner (Fred) Shoe Shop, *138*
Werner's Hill, *6*
West Coast Theatre Company, 45
Whalen, John, 32-33
White, Edward, 78, 83
White, Horace, 52
White House, The, 98
White, Hugh C., 31
White, W. A., 63
White, W. H., 87
Whitsitt, Sylvester, 32, 35, 126
Wickersham, Florilla, *135*
Willets, L. V., 61
Williams, Jim, 122
Williamson, John, 122
Wilson (Chief Engineer), 107-108
Wilson, F. A., 133
Wilson, Fred, *21*
Wilson, Willie, *59*
Windcrest Ranch Company, 77
Wittschen, Roy, 85
Wo, Chong, 72-73
Woman's Club, 29-*30*
Women's Christian Temperance Union, 36
Woolworth's, 142
Wright, T. M., 41
Wyckoff and Aston, 98
Wyckoff and Gardner, 98
Wyckoff, Cyrus Newton, 29
Wyckoff, Frank, 29
Wyckoff, Ralph, 19, 30-31, 66

Young's Coffee Store, 101

Zar Brothers, 77
Zar Saloon, 45, *48*
Zar, Stella, 88